CR_EAT^E!

Developing *Your* Creative Process

ICSC Press
International Center for Studies in Creativity
SUNY Buffalo State
1300 Elmwood Avenue, Chase 244
Buffalo, New York 14222

Library of Congress Control Number: 2020943084

Cover design by Paul Reali, photo by Diogenes Garzon on Unsplash
Interior design by Melissa Schropp
Author photo by Libby Dickinson

ISBN: 978-1-7348618-0-8 (paperback)
Also available in ebook formats
icscpress.com/books/create

CREATE!

Developing *Your* Creative Process

Cathy Pickens

ICSC Press

International Center *for*
Studies *in* Creativity

Buffalo State · The State University of New York

Contents

Chapter 1
Creative? ...Enough?

"I don't have a creative bone in my body."
— a salesman

"I used to love to play the guitar, but I haven't done that in years."
— a banker

"I have lots of great ideas, but I can't seem to get anything finished."
— a graphic designer

"I know I'm creative. But it's not always there when I need it."
— a writer

"I'm getting old. How can I keep my brain alive?"
— everyone, at a certain age

A few years ago, if you'd asked me, "Are you creative?" I'd have given you a confused smile. Creative? No. A good worker bee. Drawn to words and pictures and colors and stories. Love to write and dance and play music and work with thread or wood. But no, not particularly creative.

You see, I know creative people. Really creative people. They're dazzling. Sparks shoot off them. They're brilliant. What they make stuns the breath from my body.

No, I'd say, I'm not that.

Then one day, lightning struck. My path shifted directions, opened up. I found the happy collision of two sides of my life and, in that intersection, I found the definition of genuine creativity— a creativity that lives in each one of us.

Did you hear me? Each. One. All of us. Everybody.

How can I be so sure? After the lightning strike, I spent years studying the creativity research, as any nerd would. As a creative person, I played and lived with it, testing its limits. Now I can lay it out for you—the whole path, so you can try it and decide for yourself.

These techniques let you feed and use your creativity all the time, not just in random bursts. You can live a creative life—no matter what you do or where you use it.

In exploring what it means to be creative, I did what creative people do: I observed, asked questions, listened. One listening post was my family stories. My grandparents were hardy Southern Appalachian Scots-Irish farmers. They created from necessity; they spun and wove cloth, built furniture and houses. Pappy rigged a water-powered generator, gravity-fed from the stone cistern he'd built up the hill. It heated water by routing it around the fireplace and even supplied enough electricity to provide a bit of light. But he likely thought being "creative" sounded frivolous.

For entertainment, my grandparents sang, wrote poetry, played instruments, hooked rugs (three of those ended up in the

Eisenhower White House). A photograph of my paternal grand-parents graced the cover of Common Threads, a 1993 remake of Eagles' songs. How Granny hated that photo! Taken during the Great Depression by a traveling photographer, it showed them dying yarn. The photographer wanted her and Pappy to look like poor mountain folk. Granny had no nostalgia for such as that.

If anyone had ever asked, "Are you creative?" my kinfolk would have replied with a puzzled look and a shake of the head. No, they wouldn't describe themselves as creative—not my parents, none of my grandparents, not even my sisters (whose talents include music, quilting and sewing, interior design, and making rocking chairs and teddy bears). They're just being what they are, doing what presents itself to them to do.

It took a while, but I realized where I'd gotten my definition of myself: I was a craftsman-like worker because that was how my grandparents and my parents would've described themselves.

I've found I wasn't alone, stuck in a definition much too nar-row, too confining. Most of us don't understand the depth and reach of our creative abilities. Being creative is a given. But even those who know they're creative don't always know how to har-ness it. In short, claiming and using our creative abilities—that's the secret and the challenge.

> "To create means to relate. The root meaning of the word art is to fit together, and we all do this every day. Not all of us are painters but we are all artists. Each time we fit things together we are creating—whether it is to make a loaf of bread, a child, or a day."
>
> Corita Kent and Jan Steward, artists

So, What Does it Mean to be Creative?

Creation addresses a need—sometimes an artistic need (as when a breathtaking landscape prompts a photographer or painter to attempt to capture the image) or a practical one (as when a machinist designs a faster or safer way to transport materials). The process starts with something that needs to be new. At its heart, to create is to make something, to bring it into being.

Instead of asking whether you are creative, the better question is whether you act creative. Do you make or do or solve things? Saying "I'm a writer" doesn't make me a writer. Writing makes me a writer. Creative problem-solving makes me a different, more creative leader.

Putting together a dinner party, a charity fundraiser, a game for children, or an outfit for an interview—all creative acts. We do them every day. The only question here: can we do them better? More consistently? More brilliantly?

So, when I talk about "artists" or "creatives," I'm talking about all of us who develop and use our abilities, in whatever field.

> "All human life is filled with works of art of every kind, from cradle song, jest, mimicry, the ornamentation of houses, dresses and utensils, up to church services, buildings, monuments and triumphal processions."
> — Leo Tolstoy in What is Art?

The CREATE! Process

Is there a creative *process?* Yes. A process is simply a series of steps taken toward a particular end. A process offers structure and discipline, which can help you understand where you are and what you might be missing, where you get stuck and what comes next. Those creating in a lot of different disciplines have tested this roadmap, so why not see what a little structure and discipline can add to *your* creative work.

> "[Those] who are successful at producing truly innovative work are masters at controlling the process."
>
> Mark Oldach, graphic designer

Books that promise to help solve a problem or uncover a new path and then take forever getting there frustrate me. Before we explore how you'll use your amped-up creative abilities, let's jump right to the CREATE! process itself. Then we'll look at how to figure out for yourself what you'll do with your superpowers.

CREATE is an acronym:

- ❑ Capture
- ❑ Ramble
- ❑ Engage
- ❑ Act
- ❑ Tweak
- ❑ Expand

Let's explore in detail what those words mean.

T H E
C R E A T E !
P R O C E S S

C = CAPTURE

See a problem to solve, situation to improve, something to build on. Generate, recognize, and capture ideas. Observe, gather, connect, learn, see, hear, ask. Collect it all in a notebook, talk to yourself about it on paper. Find quiet time for thinking deeply.

R = RAMBLE

Be aware and mindful. Be curious. Indulge in experiences. Remember how to play. Dig deep into what you think you know. From experts, learn anew what you already know. Learn in areas unknown and unfamiliar. Look for connections. See things with childlike eyes.

E = ENGAGE

Settle in. Decide what you want to master. Move from play toward mastery. Focus on a particular field or project. Develop ideas. Plan. Wrestle your ideas into shape.

A = ACT

Commit the time and space. Commit yourself. Develop a routine. Struggle to get started. Start anyway. Overcome fear, inertia, or constraints. Know eureka moments don't happen by accident. Dive in and do it, write it, paint it, design it, try it, make it.

T = TWEAK

Evaluate what works and what doesn't. Live with it, walk all around it. Learn to trust your judgment. Fail. Do it again, better. Invite others to evaluate and critique it; learn the art of finding those special people. Learn to give constructive critique as well as how to receive and use it.

E = EXPAND

Move from one creative project to the next. Expand from a project to living a creative life. Recognize and support creativity in others.

The CREATE! process isn't linear; you may need to revisit steps as you work through a project. You may stay in the "playful" stages (capture and ramble) for a long time, until you settle on a particular project (where you engage and act). Tweak will invariably send you back to reconsider things. Knowing where you are on the roadmap can help you identify what bogs you down and how to move past a bog.

The Wizard of Oz is my all-time favorite movie. Maybe it's because I really believe there's no place like home. Or maybe it's because I believe, in the magical land of the creative, we find out that, all along, we had the gifts we longed for: a heart to feel and understand, a brain to think, and the courage to make it come true. You have what it takes. The CREATE! process will be your yellow brick road. Enjoy the journey.

Chapter 2

Notes For Naysayers

Even those trained in the traditional arts don't always know what they know; they may not understand the process in their work. Some of us aren't disciplined. Some of us don't take criticism well. Others understand discipline, but we won't let ourselves play or make mistakes.

To be successfully creative, we have to explore along a lot of continuums, work through some doubts, and find our own rhythms. We must be willing to be open, to take risks.

Left or Right?

The most frequent challenge I've heard from those first exploring? *I'm not really creative. I'm more of a left-brain person.*

We are so certain people are either born creative or they aren't that we even have slang terms for it: left-brain thinkers are logical and practical; right-brain thinkers are creative.

Our brains do have two sides, and each side controls unique functions. Our left brain is logical, linear, analytical, and our right brain is peripatetic, emotional, conceptual, creative. But the two sides need each other. After all, my résumé skews distinctly "left"-brained: finance major, lawyer, business school professor, university administrator. But I've also paid bills as a writer, dancer, and musician.

The real split exists not between left-brainers and right-brainers, but between those who have developed their creative abilities and those who haven't. We can develop our two-sided abilities—and, in the process, help make our lives whole.

To apply what successful "right-brainers" or "artists" know in traditionally "un-artistic" fields requires a broad definition of "artist." My broad definition? Artists are those people in any field—electrical engineering, music, teaching, parenting, shipbuilding—who understand and use their creative abilities.

If you want more on the brain science of why this can work for you, turn to Appendix I: Brain Owners' Quick-Start Guide. Or trust me that it works, keep reading, and study that later.

> "Everybody is creative, and everybody is talented. I just don't think everybody is disciplined."
> Al Hirshfield, cartoonist

Some are More So...

The other most common challenge from naysayers? *Sure, we're all creative. But some people are more so...aren't they?*

Yes...and no.

> "Genius is one percent inspiration and ninety-nine percent perspiration."
> Thomas Edison, inventor

Creative abilities fall along a continuum, and the Michelangelos, Michael Jordans, or Albert Einsteins of the creative world are rare, it is true. How can we possibly measure up, on a list of traits or accomplishments, with the truly gifted? We are all creative, but how creative is creative enough?

On the other hand, why should someone else's greater talent keep us from enjoying ours? As one workshop student observed, "I'll never play tennis like Serena Williams, but I still love playing. So why did I stop singing just because I'll never be on *American Idol*?"

We listen too much to what others say. And most of us give too much credit to personal traits and too little to hard work.*

I need to speak aloud one ugly, unspoken secret. Let's admit that what we call "success" is dangerous. Chasing success can fail to motivate us. In our rock-star culture, we link creativity with money and fame, popularity and success. One reason we fail to recognize our own creativity is that many creative solutions are small, with limited application, though they are nonetheless elegant and useful and an improvement in our lives or those of others.

---

*Much has been written about the 10,000-hour rule—that you can master anything if you do it for 10,000 hours, that work ethic explains more than talent. [See research by psychologist K. Anders Ericksson, popularized in *Talent is Overrated: What Really Separates World-Class Performers from Everybody Else*, Geoff Colvin (2008/2010); *The Genius in All of Us*, David Shenk (2010); and *Outliers: The Story of Success*, Malcolm Gladwell (2008).] Does that mean you can be a genius? If you start early enough and work hard enough, maybe yes.

But let's be realistic. Muggsy Bogues played professional basketball as a guard with the NBA—at 5'3" tall. That's how tall I am. Does that mean, if I work hard enough, I can play professional basketball? Unequivocally—no. Why? Putting aside the very real musculoskeletal differences between me and Muggsy, I didn't start early enough, work hard enough, or—and this is important—want it badly enough. That's the real lesson behind all the hype about the 10,000-hour rule: those with even moderate abilities can succeed if they work hard enough. To really become proficient as, say, a violinist or athlete, physical realities mean you have to start young to get your 10,000 hours in. Does that mean you should give up your dreams because you're older? Maybe you need to recalibrate your dreams, but give them up? Please don't. You know better than that.

This 10,000-hours notion always sparks lots of discussion. The research and illustrations are interesting and beyond the scope of this book. But at its heart, there's plenty of evidence that hard work pays off—and also evidence that real talent can lie fallow and be wasted.

> "Success is a consequence
> and must not be a goal."
> Gustave Flaubert, writer

But we may discount those creative acts because they did not make us rich or famous. And that is what worthy creative acts are supposed to do, isn't it? Lead to fame and fortune? That expectation may derail more budding creative acts than anything else. After all, why write a novel or sing a song if you know you'll never top the charts? That's why Madeleine L'Engle, author of *A Wrinkle in Time*, called success "one of the dirtiest temptations of the devil."

Of course, everyone enjoys recognition—that is a strong motivator. But making music or painting a picture for your own enjoyment should be as worthy an act in developing your creative process as a Carnegie Hall performance or a painting displayed at MOMA. Your work may garner fewer admirers, it is true. But the path that led to the final product is the same—and just as enriching and motivating.

Of course we want to create something that will leave the world—or our boss or parents or spouse or friends—speechless with awe, delight, and envy. We want to be successful. But if success is your primary goal, you will inevitably fall short. Your reward must be the process of creating, not how the product is received. Looking too far down the road to the end game, to the product, to *The New York Times* bestseller list, or to your promotion to the corner office will distract you, cause you to lose focus or put your focus on the wrong things, encourage short-cuts, and ultimately frustrate you. What you see as the pinnacles of success will prove, in the long run, fickle and false.

Love the work itself, find your passion in solving the problem, addressing the need, answering the question, and you'll find a lifetime of passion and energy. And maybe, just maybe, success.

> "Persistence trumps talent every time."
> Cathy Pickens

Care and Feeding of a Whole Brain

What have I learned about being a creative person in a "left-brained" career? The ability to use the creative process is:

❑ **UNIVERSAL.** Everyone is creative. Everyone. The question isn't, "Am I creative?" No, better questions are, "Have I developed my creativity?" or "Do I use it?" No two people are creative in the same way. Some don't recognize their ability. Most of us never use it to its full potential. But it's part of the prize package for being born human.

❑ **DISCIPLINED**…and magical. The creative process doesn't involve sitting around waiting on a fortuitous visit from a Muse. In reality, while there is magic, it is process and discipline that brings forth the magic.

❑ **UNLIMITED.** Creativity isn't reserved only for the arts. The creative among us include technical specialists: computer designers, mathematicians, engineers. And some who love the arts do not themselves produce many creative ideas or works. To be creative requires both the idea and the output.

❑ **HARD WORK.** Expertise—as much for an engineer, an accountant, or a financial analyst as for a dancer or painter—is critical for effective creativity, and gaining expertise means investing time and energy.

❑ **CONTAGIOUS.** Creativity begets creativity. Creative people feed on the creative thoughts and actions of others. Not in a derivative, Hollywood-sequel "if it worked once, do it twenty times" way, but as a rich Petri dish for growing new, better, different ideas.

❑ **DELICATE.** Creativity is fragile. The right environment can nurture creativity even in those who don't consider themselves creative. The wrong environment can kill creativity—or at least force it underground—in even the most naturally creative people.

❑ **PLAYFUL.** Experiment is just as important as expertise. Artists know how to play—with ideas, with situations, with new views of old problems, with life. The freedom to try new combinations, to play with child-like abandon, is one of the first traits squelched by modern life, starting with elementary school. Play is also one of the magical doors opening into a creative life.

ॐ

The steps in the CREATE! process introduce you to each of these elements. But the steps are not passive. You cannot just read about being creative, you have to create. Create is an action verb. Ready to get busy?

Chapter 3

Capture (and Cogitate)

> "The moment we realize that any thought, ours or borrowed, is pregnant enough not to be wasted, or original enough not to be likely to come back again, we must fix it on paper."
>
> Ernest Dimnet, "The Art of Thinking"

Some of the skills needed to live a creative life are so commonplace, such regular parts of our lives, that we tend to dismiss them or check them off our list too quickly. When I ask writers and other artists, "Do you keep a notebook or journal?" the common response is a nod of the head, often a dismissive *of course I do* wave of the hand. Jotting stuff in a notebook is *de rigueur* for a writer, isn't it?

With my next questions, the answers are often more sober or reluctant: How do you use your notebook to develop ideas? How deliberate or purposeful is your notebook?

Ideas float by every day, but do we focus on them? Capture them? Develop them? Do we take time to cogitate—to "take careful thought or think carefully about: ponder"?*

Of course you come up with ideas, but how deeply and differently do you think? And do you capture your ideas in a usable fashion?

We often take our ideas for granted and therefore fail to devote the time or develop techniques that can help us do it better.

Idea Capture

Despite my intense personal belief about the importance of a notebook, I was at first reluctant to recommend that others keep one. I was reluctant despite the fact I know it is a critical part of my creative process. I was reluctant because I feared it was a powerful technique only for those who create in a world of words. Is it, I wondered, as effective for those who create in science or business or...dance?

I am reluctant no longer. Keeping a notebook can be one of the most powerful tools in your creativity toolbox, no matter what you create or how.

Why am I so certain? Because many types of artists, scientists, and others have kept notebooks; some of these notebooks have become well-known works in their own right. Naturalists (Emerson), painters (Degas), sculptors (Michelangelo and da Vinci, with his books full of reverse writing and line sketches), inventors (Edison, with his detailed five million notebook pages), dancers (Martha Graham, Twyla Tharp), military strategists (Marcus Aurelius), and others all kept notebooks. They all talked about the

---

* American Heritage Dictionary

vital necessity of their notebooks in their creative lives. I've also read the first notebooks of my students and gotten reports from consulting clients as they began to use notebooks in their creative process. In all these cases, it is powerful tool—and addictive.

Interestingly enough, this initial step on the creative path is also the juncture at which many creative people push back. The good news is, in my experience, those who shy away from the idea of a journal or notebook are often the ones who unlock its deep significance and master its usefulness better than those who respond, "Oh, boy! I love journaling." I can't explain why, I've just seen it happen too often to discount it. Maybe the reluctant ones work harder at finding its meaning. Maybe those who have kept journals in the past fall too easily into old habits without trying new, potentially more productive techniques.

I shy away from the terms "journal" or "diary" because those carry images either of the hearts-and-flowers page-a-day books with golden locks and keys favored by little girls—and their mischievous brothers. Or the terms evoke an earnest, perhaps more masculine image, of a Thomas Jefferson bowed over a weighty, leather-bound tome. "Journal" and "diary" also carry a commitment; both terms, at their root, mean "daily." That is a heavy commitment. The thought that one is required to write in a notebook every day has a paralytic effect. "I'm too busy! I have *real* work to do! How can I possibly manage one more thing?"

Keeping a notebook may seem an unnatural act at first—either too juvenile, too pedestrian, or too demanding—but regular writing is a skill worth developing. And it doesn't have to be a burden.

Any serious creator will attest to the fleeting nature of ideas. Whatever your field, whatever you are working on, new connections, ideas, or directions will pop up at the oddest times and places. Be ready. You won't remember.

> "'I'll never forget this' is the devil's whisper. Catch everything that matters in your notebook."
> Richard Bach, author

For me, an idea can circle my brain like a hamster in its plastic play ball, rolling helter-skelter, never quite lighting anywhere, never quite finished. I have to write the idea to fix it in place.

> "Unless you catch ideas on the wing and nail them down, you soon cease to have any."
> Virginia Woolf

Once it is fixed in place, I can analyze it, see where it might fit, tinker with it, build on it, discard it and move on…or return to it, sometimes years later.

That passage of time itself can be an important element in the process. As Thomas Mallon in his study of diarists found, reading what you've captured over a period of time illustrates "the sporadic visitings of creativity." Sporadic? Yes. Worth capturing, just in case? Certainly. Seeing similar ideas or the same themes emerging—sometimes separated by years—tells you something about where you need to focus your energies.

The ritual of keeping a notebook also makes articulating your ideas easier. Writer Katherine Mansfield, whose notebooks were a jumble of shopping lists, drafts of letters, and reading lists, said: "It's very strange, but the mere act of writing anything is a help. It seems to speed one on one's way."

"When my brain gets 'clogged,' then I just find a piece of paper and start to write to unclog it. Since I started keeping a notebook, I find I am also writing more as part of my job. About a month ago, a colleague asked me to write something up for her. Normally I would have not even given it a try, but now I do. I am not a great writer but I am not afraid of writing like I used to be. That is a start."

B.M., workshop student

A notebook is also useful to keep project outlines, contacts, meeting summaries, and the like. A former banker told me he always carries a small Moleskine notebook; one of his notebooks contains the initial plan for the entrepreneurial venture he now operates, jotted down when it was only an idea and long before it became reality. Graphic designer Mark Oldach recommended writing down everything a client says in interviews: "As the client talks, your ideas are already flowing." But those idea sparks may die out if not captured.

From my experience, from that of my workshop students, and from centuries of creative lives, of this I am certain: You must experiment seriously with capturing your ideas on paper and seeing what you think. You must commit to the experiment for enough time to acquire the habit and see the results. You will develop your own methods and what works best for you. And it will work. Without this tool, though, your creative process is crippled.

Let me be frank: If you are not willing to try keeping a notebook, you may as well abandon reading this book and move on to some other endeavor. That's how important keeping a notebook can be to your creative process. True, notebooks don't serve everyone's needs or work in every stage of our creative lives, but abandon your experiment only after you've given it a serious attempt—at least sixty days (the length of time, studies show, to develop a new habit).

Communing With Yourself

We usually write to transmit our ideas to others. However, by the time we're ready to transmit ideas, those ideas are already "thought" and only need organization and translation.

But writing has another, often underrated function. Writing can help us think, explore options, discover connections we haven't consciously recognized yet.

Some of us—even some who call ourselves writers—shy away from writing because, somewhere along the way, we had all the fun sucked out of putting words on paper. And we've never gotten it back. We were taught that a command of grammar rules makes one a good writer. No mistake about it—grammar rules are important. To communicate with others, our writing needs structure. As with rules of etiquette or rules of the road, grammar rules smooth our interactions with others. But rules alone don't make you a good driver, a good host—or a good writer or thinker.

For now, forget writing to communicate with others. Instead, talk to yourself. Use writing as a tool to help you focus and think. When writing to think, you make the rules to suit yourself. Experiment. But you must commit to try it for long enough to discover what works for you.

If you hate to write, think of this as "scribbling." To scribble effectively, you don't have to consider yourself a "writer." No one else will read your notebook, so relax and enjoy it. Then, when you are ready to communicate, you'll know what you think and you'll have fresh ideas to share.

I've seen an amazing side benefit to keeping a notebook: even for those who struggle to express themselves in writing, keeping a notebook actually improves their ability to write, not just when they are writing for themselves but also when they later write to be read.

Even if you're skeptical about whether it will work for you, try it. For two months, write something every day. Then you can alter, adapt, stop. But first, give it a try.

Choosing Your Tools

Does a notebook have a certain form? No, but tools in any creative endeavor are important—important in part because "form ever follows function," as architect Louis Sullivan said. In the act of creating, form may dictate outcome.

When speaking at a library event, I met a woman who had always loved to write. In grammar school, though, her father had cautioned her not to waste her school notebooks, so she scrimped three lines of writing into every line of her paper, to make each notebook last longer. She told me the story with a smile on her face as she clutched a battered spiral notebook. She leaned close, with a conspiratorial grin. "I use a whole line now," she said. Her story taught me much about respecting our tools—and cherishing an abundance of paper.

Natalie Goldberg, author of *Writing Down the Bones,* likes cheap spiral-bound school theme books so she can scribble away and not feel constrained by the demands of expensive paper.

When I began regularly keeping a notebook in college, I jotted notes on 3x5 note cards or handy scraps of paper, to be transcribed into a notebook later. That became a chore and, like too many chores, often put off to the point where I couldn't remember what the cryptic scribble meant. So I moved to a small Moleskine notebook that fit in my very small purse or in a jacket pocket; with the notebook, I could flesh out an idea more fully in spare moments. Frankly, that little notebook's highest purpose became protecting me from boredom: sitting on a bench after touring London's Imperial War Museum while my husband read every display card in the place, or waiting for a delayed meeting to start, or during a speech, whether it was irritating or inspiring me.

For a time, I used small 6x9 three-ring binders so I could add and subtract tabs and move things around. Some writers worry that loose-leaf pages may too easily be lost, but if I could readily find heavy, smooth binder paper in this size, I might use that format exclusively. However, I also like having thoughts bound, since I have what I call "positional memory." I remember where things are by where I first put them and like seeing things in the context in which they were collected.

I now carry a bound notebook—typically 5x7 or 6x8. I learned to avoid notebooks with thin or rough paper or ones that don't lay flat. I love smooth, thick paper and wide, generous lines.

A cupboard in my study holds notebooks of all shapes and sizes, filled with scribbles. I like variety.

I am picky about my pens, too. Levenger's True Writer, especially the "bold" ballpoint, is a favorite, or the Schmidt "Parker Style" refills. And I've recently succumbed to the charms of a fountain pen. Pilot's Varsity disposable medium point is a good starter pen, and I am now a TWSBI addict.

Your notebook can have cats on the cover or can be a collection of scribbled napkins from McDonald's that you stapled together. Cheap spiral notebook, fine Italian leather journal, word processing file, sketch paper, Bic or MontBlanc, a mechanical pencil on a quadrille pad. Whatever suits you. You will probably change from time to time. Good tools show respect for the process and for your ideas, but don't get tools that are so dear you are afraid to use them. Pick tools you enjoy, and be willing to experiment.

Do think carefully about a couple of options, especially before you invest a lot of money in an expensive notebook. What size page do you want? Too small may feel too cramped; too large and it can't be carried easily or surreptitiously pulled out.

Decide if you want blank pages or lined. Visual artists often prefer blank pages so they can sketch as well as write without feeling constrained by lines. I prefer lined paper, but narrow lines are too cramped for my handwriting.

The only thing that matters is that you use your notebook enough to get good at it, to know what it can do, so it becomes a natural part of your creative process, one you rely on with ease.

☞ POST-IT POEMS. Former North Carolina Poet Laureate Cathy Smith Bowers is a gifted teacher. When she talks about her art and about her students, her enthusiasm is contagious. She was telling me how fascinated she was with a student who wrote rich, dense, compact poems. One day, when the student came to talk about a work-in-progress, Cathy saw clearly how form could affect product: the student drafted her poems on three-inch Post-It notepads!

Building Your Notebook

The first step is to get a notebook and a pen (or pencil). You may later switch to typing your journal, but start by handwriting it.

I must admit, I have a bias in favor of handwritten notebooks, even though I at times also use a keyboard for the same purpose—exploration, idea capture, idle chit-chat with myself. I don't think it's an irrational bias. Recent research about the shift away from teaching cursive writing is exploring how handwriting activates certain sectors of the brain. Not definitive scientific support for my bias, I admit, but I know it works. For me, watching words flow over the page is organic. Notebooks and pens are also very portable, don't have to be turned off for airplane take-offs and landings, and can even be used unobtrusively during sermons or while waiting on the bus.

You can jot notes or talk to yourself (on paper, that is) while waiting for a colleague or in the dentist's waiting room. No need to boot up. Never a low battery. You can even be discreetly working out an idea during a really boring meeting; just make sure you look up and nod at appropriate intervals, so it looks as though you are taking notes. If your handwriting is as bad as mine, no one can read it over your shoulder.

As a practical matter, most people dictate more than twice as fast as they can type, and most type twice as fast as they can write by hand. Therefore, a handwritten notebook slows you down and lets you process thoughts as you write.

You may want to mix it up. Writer Anne Hazard Aldrich said, "It is important for me to write poems and songs by hand. I write prose with a typewriter (a computer) but I must write the things that have a flow of phrasing and an immediacy by hand." I typically write fiction by hand and nonfiction on a laptop.

I acknowledge my bias and believe it is not purely arbitrary or archaic. That said, use whatever method works for you. Or methods. At times, I switch to a keyboard because thoughts are coming quickly and are already well-formed. I don't need to think much, just transcribe. I then print the pages and put them in a binder that I keep in addition to whatever bound notebook I'm carrying around at the time.

☞ THE ELECTRONIC WORKING JOURNAL. Sue Grafton, best-selling novelist, kept an electronic working journal alongside each novel. Her process is worth investigating. She had long been a student of Jungian psychology, one of the branches that most draws on journaling as a means of self-exploration. She began each writing day by opening the computer file containing her journal for that book. Talking to herself opened up the creative flow; she saw it as allowing her left and right brains or her Jungian Ego (public self) and Shadow (private self) to talk to each other. "The journal is experimental," she said. "The journal functions as a playground for the mind, a haven where the imagination can cavort at will."

She used her electronic journal to talk about how to resolve issues in that day's writing. Sometimes she copied whole sections from the journal into the book manuscript because she'd had a breakthrough and the story had begun to flow. Her journal could be four times longer than the book itself, when she finished.

Like Sue Grafton, I talk to myself before I start a day's writing. Rather than a keyboard, I prefer smooth, heavy, lined paper and a pen. I want it to flow, dark and thick. I handwrite my first fiction drafts in a large stitched notebook, though nonfiction starts out on the computer. I can't tell you why the distinction. When I start a day of fiction writing, I scribble on the back of the notebook page on which yesterday's writing ended. Sometimes I have a lot to purge—frustrations, plans, things I'm trying to process, looking forward to, or dreading. Sometimes I'm just in a chatty mood and don't really want to get down to work. This may take a paragraph or it can travel along the backs of several pages before I'm ready to start the real work of writing, on the fronts of the pages. Eventually, though, the extraneous bits are cleared out of my head and I can get down to work. The words are flowing.

One or Many?

Notebook-keepers often debate whether to keep separate work and personal notebooks, or a notebook for each project, or a separate book for quotes and ephemera and notes on books read. Or should it just jumble all together in one notebook?

Tristine Rainer, in *The New Diary*, did not like the idea of separate notebooks for different purposes. She liked it all jumbled together, so she could see what was interesting her and affecting her at a particular time. She wanted integration, which is a worthy goal; integration unifies us, makes us whole, gives us a sense of purpose and, eventually, completion.

I found a compromise: I keep almost everything in one notebook now, divided into sections with little stick-on flags or tabs. The first half is for scribbling or daily writing. Random chats with myself, warm-ups for a project, venting, talking to myself about how best to approach something or organize my time.

I rarely read back over the first section of my notebooks, the "daily writing" section that is most like a traditional "journal." The writing itself served its one-time purpose.

The other sections contain information for projects, so I find it helpful not to have to wade through too much chatty irrelevance to find what I need. The second section, about one-quarter of the notebook, works as a mini-project notebook and collects story or article ideas. Some are references to something I've read or seen on television or in a newspaper. Some are fleshed-out plot ideas or character sketches or lecture ideas.

The last quarter of the notebook is for detailed notes on books I've read—often research on crime cases, because I write about historic cases and because I'm fascinated by the subject.

I also keep a separate devotional notebook where I write meditations or jot notes from readings. That's a notebook I'll return to in the future for a single purpose, so I no longer mix it up with everything else. I also sometimes carry a small, pocket-sized notebook or notecards, just in case.

It took some years and several notebooks for me to figure out what I needed and could best use. And I'm sure it will change again.

All this to say, do what works for you. Play with it. Let it flow together, keep separate notebooks, use a loose-leaf system. Experiment and decide for yourself.

Others' Notebooks

Your notebook will serve different purposes for you, at different times, just as notebooks have in the lives of famous notebook-keepers. The first published diary opened in January 1660, with Samuel Pepys' words, "Bless be God, at the end of the last year I was in very good health...." Until 1667, he recorded events that ranged from dinner at his house and his sexual dalliances with women to the world-changing 1666 Great Fire of London and the Black Plague. Is it that writers involved in grand events feel compelled to record them? Or does the recording of those events preserve them, elevating their status? Pepys never expected anyone to read his diary, but it is still in print over 300 years later; his personal reactions to what might be dry history keep it readable today.

Prior to the Renaissance, with its creative awakening and spread of education, most journal-keepers were clergy (as in Saint Augustine's 4th century *Confessions*). As travel opened up unexplored lands, travelers recorded their discoveries for themselves and for those who would never see the sights firsthand.

Pre-dating all of these, Marcus Aurelius penned his *Meditations*. Circa 167 A.D., the emperor perched on his camp stool late into the night, using his quill and ink to explore the meaning of his life in words that resonate centuries later and far removed from the deprivations of a military campaign: "Nothing has such power to broaden the mind as the ability to investigate systematically and truly all that comes under thy observation in life."

In *A Book of One's Own*, an exploration of diaries, professor Thomas Mallon made distinctions between commonplace books or notebooks, on one hand, and diaries or journals. He considered diaries "higher order" because they were more introspective and more narrative. He suggested that the diarist often anticipates it will be read by someone at some point and writes with that imagined audience in mind.

For artists, notebooks are workbooks. Even though an artist's notebook may also record events, grand and personal, or serve as a psychological outlet, at its heart it is "a private fragmentary scribble book," according to journaling coach Burghild Nina Holzer.

An artist's notebook isn't something the artist expects anyone else to read. It is therefore not self-conscious. It is not introspective or navel-gazing (necessarily). It is a repository. It is a *work book*. It serves the creator and no one else. In fact, it is often indecipherable to anyone else.

Making Time

To make the most of a creative notebook, you must first clear away a space in your life for it. Your life is already jammed to the rafters, you say? Of course it is. But a key part of the creative process is the time to think—enough time, on a regular basis.

However, you don't need to quit your job, abandon your family, and renounce personal hygiene. It takes about fifteen minutes to fill a page (about 250 words, handwritten), so identify fifteen to thirty minutes a day for your notebook. You will find this a gracious plenty. Eventually, you will also find more time. I guarantee it. (And eventually, you'll use some of this "found" time on your creative projects.)

Be deliberate and make a very specific commitment with yourself. Put it on your calendar. Many write early in the morning. A friend of mine records life at the end of every day; interestingly, he's an historian by training.

Small amounts of time add up, but without time, you'll have no creative activity. You don't need a whole day (even though having one is great). Face it, just as you can't launch right into a three-hour gym workout, you also won't be able to make the best use of huge blocks of time as you begin your creative workouts. For one thing, large blocks of time and lofty goals can be intimidating. Start with what you know you can manage.

> "In order to let my creative process flow, I must have time to think and reflect. My tendency is not to allow myself time to do this. I literally have to force myself to just stop and be still."
>
> — R.B, workshop student

How to find the first fifteen minutes? Keep a log of how you spend your time every day, in half-hour or fifteen-minute increments. What can you cut out? Thoreau noted, "Our life is frittered away by detail.... Simplify, simplify." Will anyone die if you dust-mop up the dog hair only every other day? Or maybe one of your children is ready for that chore? Eliminate. Delegate. Postpone.

Maybe your daily writing works best as part of your daily time management system or your meditation time. For some scribblers, morning is best, before coffee or anyone else wakes up. Maybe you do it during your morning bus trip or during your lunch break in the park or while waiting in the carpool line.

Identify your main distractions. For too many of us, "screen time" is a waste of time. Will you get as much from thirty minutes watching TV or surfing social sites as you will from capturing and developing ideas on paper? Probably not. Eliminate distractions and time-wasters.

But what I do is important, you say, even vital. Perhaps it is, but analyze it carefully. Is it really? As Roman philosopher Seneca explained, "Every one has time if he likes. Business runs after nobody; people cling to it of their own free will and think that to be busy is proof of happiness."

To what are you clinging? What can you let go? So few of us are truly indispensible, no matter how much we love to believe otherwise.

Maybe your best hope is to set the clock a half an hour earlier or postpone bedtime. I hate to recommend these, since statistics say you get too little sleep as it is.

Only you can make time for this. The benefit will be that you will find it easier, the more you do it. Time is, after all, an elastic concept.

The consistency of your routine is important as you begin to use this tool. At first, develop a daily habit until you learn what works best for you. "If you skip a day or two, it is hard to get started again," said writing teacher Brenda Ueland. "In a queer way, you are afraid of it. It takes again an hour or two of vacant noodling, when nothing at all comes out on paper, and this is difficult always because it makes us busy, efficient Anglo-Saxons with our accomplishment mania, feel uneasy and guilty." This mania is contagious and has spread in our culture beyond the Anglo-Saxon among us.

After you see what regularly keeping a notebook can do for you, you may scribble every day or only sporadically. But if you only scribble sporadically, your ideas won't flow as easily and you will take longer to "warm up." Like exercising at the gym, scribbling—and cogitating—strengthens only with regularity. You will find the habit pays dividends.

Aside from capturing ideas you can return to and develop, you will find another important dividend from keeping your notebook. You will also find yourself more aware, more mindful, more focused. Even when you aren't writing, you'll be thinking about what you'd like to capture or explore. Mindfulness and focus are critical components in the creative process. You will find yourself developing these skills along with your idea capture and idea development skills. These are pretty good dividends for investing fifteen minutes a day!

> "I have a greater awareness of creativity and how it applies to my everyday life. I look for creativity in different places now. How are we creative at work? What things stand in the way of our creativity? How can I approach my problems and struggles differently? I realized I haven't been using creativity as a tool in my life. In a way I let creativity atrophy in my life."
>
> — R.B., workshop student

But What Will I Write?

Many who approach a notebook for the first time get a pinched expression, their hands tightened into fists: "But what will I write about?"

"Anything you want," is far from a reassuring response. In fact, that response typically produces even more anxiety.

Sitting down with your notebook and pen and just starting is the best technique. You can write "This is dumb. I don't know what to write." You can write about why this is nerve-wracking.

Consider a parallel circumstance. Chatting with your neighbors or office mates has immeasurable benefit, adding ease and pleasure to your life at home or work—yet you rarely approach these casual chats with lofty goals. Just as casual water-cooler chats butter the bread of human discourse, chatting with yourself in your notebook will improve your ability to understand how and why you think and work.

In your notebook, talk to yourself about what's happening in the news, what you'd like to see happen in your life or career, what you are learning in classes or training, what you've learned about yourself by watching others, what connections you can make between what you're reading—fiction or nonfiction—and your work. Again, it helps to see what you are thinking.

Use it as a commonplace book, where you copy quotations or anecdotes. These can provide an inspiration for a presentation or an article or simply reassurance when you thumb back through them later.

Ask yourself questions and answer them. What results do I want from this project? What opening would grab my boss's or editor's attention? Where do I want to be in five years? Why does

X keep popping into my head? What are some wacky ways to attract more readers or customers? Asking questions will jump-start your writing—and your thinking.

Record your accomplishments. We make "to-do" lists, but what about keeping a "have done" list? Or a "stop doing" list? Record your reactions to things and capture sensory details; these expand your ability to observe and make connections. How you use your notebook will change, will become your own.

A word of advice: Date the entries. Include references or sources, in case you want to refer to or quote something later.

You may find it helpful to think about your writing—and your notebook—in at least two stages or sections: daily writing (or scribbling) and project writing (or idea capture).

Daily writing or "scribbling" makes writing feel familiar and flow more smoothly. As a side benefit, it can help you gain insights and solve problems; it also improves the ease with which you write. The benefits flow simply from the writing itself, no extra effort required.

Your scribbling doesn't need a clear purpose at first; just think of it as a brain exercise. Brenda Ueland wrote of her own "slovenly, headlong, helter-skelter diary." She said it helped show her "that writing is talking, thinking, on paper. And the more impulsive and immediate the writing the closer it is to the thinking, which it should be." She also found that scribbling helped her enjoy writing, which for years "was the most boring, dreaded, and effortful thing to do—doubt-impeded, ego-inflated."

Sometimes daily writing yields such profound insights as "This is a boring meeting." Or you may scribble "what if...?" Or "what about...?" Or "X upsets me, but I don't know why." As nutty as it may sound, these scribblings, done regularly, can dredge up useful ideas that usually float around the edges of your brain, un-captured and unformed.

Project writing will benefit from daily writing. The ritual you develop in your daily writing will train or "prime" your brain. Having a time, place, and process for regular writing gets you ready to write whenever you put yourself in that place with those tools, so ideas flow with more ease.

Over the course of several daily writing sessions, ask yourself questions about a pending project. To get the most from scribbling for a specific project, try setting aside longer uninterrupted time to "write through" problems or strategies. Particularly for larger projects, uninterrupted time is the key.

Daily Writing Techniques

The third-grader starting piano lessons will usually complain about "wasting" time on practice scales or finger exercises. "I want to play real songs, not stupid exercises." Accomplished pianists become accomplished because, somewhere along the way, they learned the value of the discipline, perhaps even learned to love the discipline, as their fingers acquired the muscle memory needed to make music.

As you develop your skills and master the habit, try some "finger exercises" to limber up:

:: Diving In ::

Brenda Ueland was a writing teacher at the YWCA in Minneapolis and counted among her friends Carl Sandburg and Eugene O'Neill. She exhorted new writers and others to "know that you have talent, are original, and have something important to say."

She advocated just diving in, letting words come. After all, this capture and cogitate phase is not the place for an editor. It is the place to explore, ask questions, play. Editing of both ideas and words comes later—much later.

Ueland has long been a favorite of mine because she helped me clearly see that capturing and analyzing are two distinct phases in the creative process. Ueland, Natalie Goldberg, and other writing coaches say just dive in, write, don't worry about getting it right. I have consciously used that image, pictured myself poised on the edge, slicing into cool blue water without effort, gliding underneath, coming up for breath far from where I started. Everything you need to buoy you and carry you along is there.

This realization was a breakthrough for me and taught me how to make better use of my notebook. Rather than simply storing the rare idea so compelling it rose to the surface and persisted in an irritating fashion until I wrote it down, I learned to loosen up and write a lot that didn't seem very important. "Diving in" helped me explore the depths, bringing up pearls—and sometimes old shoes and discarded tires—that I wouldn't have found otherwise.

:: Free-writing ::

Free-writing, recommended by professor Peter Elbow and other writing experts, is another technique to help you turn off your internal editor—another way to practice "diving in." In free-writing, set a goal to move your pen (or keyboard keys) for at least fifteen minutes. Don't stop. Don't worry about grammar or spelling. If you can't think of anything to say, write "This is REALLY stupid" over and over again. Or "What do I want to work on or write about?" Just keep writing—something will come.

This technique works well when you are generating options or narrowing down a list. But you can also use it to get comfortable talking to yourself on paper, a way to force yourself to dive in.

Once your fifteen minutes are up, read through what you've written. With a dark marker, strike out the chatter. In what remains, look for intersections, connections, broader purposes, themes. Amazingly, like a Magic 8 ball, answers will materialize from the murk. Once you see an idea in writing, your reaction will be "How simple! How obvious! Of course!" But not until it has been pulled from the subconscious and given form is it so obvious.

> "... every creative act is a sudden cessation of stupidity."
> — Edward Land, founder of Polaroid

:: Morning Pages ::

Among the best-known writing practices are morning pages, a recommendation often cited by other artists and drawn from Julia Cameron's *The Artist's Way*, a twelve-week guide to creative recovery for artists. Morning pages are an extended version of free-writing or "diving in." Every day, before you do anything else, write three pages. Handwrite, quickly, perhaps on a legal pad. Write whatever comes to mind; resolve issues from the day before; lay out the day to come; capture whatever floats to the surface.

Morning pages are an exercise, like tummy crunches. You may never read these pages again, though it can be useful to read them after a period of weeks or months. Themes will emerge, some that surprise you. Connections will become clear that you had not seen before. The premise of morning pages is that such writing frees your mind of its internal editor and allows you to draw on ideas locked in the "shadows" of your conscious mind—a Jungian concept.

Try morning pages for at least a month, preferably two. Mornings may not work best for you. You may not be able to do the pages every day; however, as with any discipline, the more routine it becomes, the more easily you slip past the "I don't want to" barrier and into the world of "this works." Most of us have the same love/hate relationship with the treadmill or weights. I don't want to start the workout, but once I do, it feels great.

My workshop students start with an average of a page a day. Some write mostly on weekends, some at night or sporadically during the day. Some do just enough to get by. Some spew out pages. Some spend part of the time complaining about having to do it—which is a legitimate use of these pages—then move on to useful ideas and question-asking. They eventually discover exactly what the exercise is designed to do: they become comfortable talking to themselves and seeing what they're thinking.

What should you write about in these pages? Anything. These are practice pages. As Cameron uses them, they are door-openers. Morning pages are the equivalent of practice scales on a piano or stretches for a runner. Morning pages may or may not be additions to your notebook. They are warm-ups, letting the words start to flow easily, in an unfiltered way. When I started, I kept these separate from my notebook, which for me is a working tool, a reference, a file for capturing and holding ideas. One writer said she burns hers, to keep the promise with herself that she can be completely truthful with herself on these pages.

In morning pages, complain about having to do them, talk about how good your coffee tastes or how it smells better than it tastes. Do as one student did almost every morning: draw a sketch of your coffee cup. Do a mind-map [see next page] of your list of things to do. Talk about why you are or aren't getting along with someone.

Modify this exercise to suit your needs. For me, the benefit of morning pages was that I felt freer just wasting time complaining and talking on paper. It became easier to do, and I now know the value of getting my brain cleared of clutter so I can move on to other things. At first, I practiced it faithfully, more faithfully than I practiced my piano scales when I was eight years old because I saw more reason to do it, but I don't write them every morning now because that doesn't suit my needs as well. Try it for yourself and see what works for you.

☛ THE CEO'S MORNING PAGES. At a workshop, the CEO of a $1.5 billion company talked about his career transition from CFO of one company to the CEO slot at another. "I realized that 'feelings' were going to be important in my new job, in a way they'd never been when I was managing financial matters. I wasn't in touch with my own responses to other people—that had not been important before. A mentor suggested I try morning pages. It sounded odd at first, but I tried it. In writing the pages over several weeks, I focused on how I felt and how others responded in situations. The surprising result was I realized my brain was actually rewiring itself. A recognition and understanding of my feelings and others' came more naturally—and made me a better leader. As crazy as it sounds, it works."

:: Mind Mapping ::

This technique can help you pull together lots of loose ends. It allows your brain to do what it does naturally—jump from one thing to another—but, at the end, you will have gathered a mass of seemingly unrelated ideas into useful order.

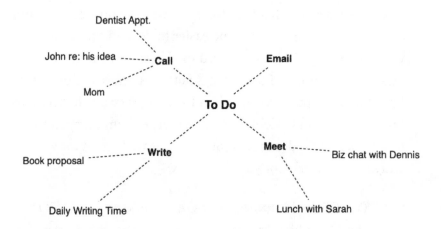

Start with a central issue or question and branch out from there. For starters, try it with your "to do" list.

As your mind jumps among unrelated topics, a Mind Map allows you to gather and consolidate those topics. You won't set priorities (which list-making implies) until you've completed the map. Then you can quickly pull together a list with priorities, and you can see associations you might otherwise miss.

Tony Buzan's *The Mind Map Book* has more complex examples, many with artwork I envy. Project management software uses mind-maps to carry this beyond the "scribbling" stage to the project stage; an online search will yield free, open-source programs as well as programs for sale.

Project Writing

Many creative people use notebooks as part of their project development routine. As part of your daily scribbling, you can collect stray thoughts, news articles, web addresses, or other sources. You can ask yourself questions or play "what if." You can test outlines or summaries or openings. When you finally sit down to write or put together a presentation, you will have collected a lot of material and will know more clearly what you think and what you want others to know or to do.

For a longer-term project, repeatedly use daily sessions to explore the same topic. For example, outline an upcoming presentation; then, several days later, outline it again, without referring back to your earlier notes. Or try out several openings or summaries for a report. Keep going back to it anew each time. Then, when you sit down to draft the report or presentation, you can choose from your best thinking and from several fresh approaches.

☛ YOUR LIFE PROJECT. Christine Comaford Lynch of venture capital firm Artemis Ventures used her notebook only a few times a year but to good effect: "It's a sitting down with my journal, and it's usually in June and December. It just works out that way. Okay. Is my life working? And there are a lot of aspects to that. Is my career life working? Is my personal life working? Am I stretching enough? What am I afraid of? Where can I go to get to the next level? Am I progressing spiritually? Am I still feeling close to God or am I getting swept up in stuff and, sliding? Yeah. I think it's so easy just to get swept up in stuff and then to wake up a few years later and go, 'Whoa, where did my life go?' So yeah, I really think it's important to assess. Hugely, hugely important."

I start every book—including this one—in just that way. I talk to myself in my notebook at random moments. Eventually each book gets its own planning notebook. I then spend concentrated time asking myself questions about what direction I want it to take, what I want to include. Every book develops in its own way, with its own successes and challenges, but each one started as I combed through my earlier notebooks and my incubator file for those random thoughts that miraculously begin to coalesce.

☛ I particularly like long plane trips—eight to ten hours is ideal. I pledge to do nothing but eat, sleep, and write. And write and write. No reading, no movies, no games. It is forced solitude, in a way. True, I could make myself work to such a grueling schedule at home, but I don't feel so imprisoned at home.

This book, incidentally, after a year of intense research, reading, and note-taking, began to take shape while my husband and I spent two cold, rainy January weeks on a train trip and in a floating house in Victoria, BC.

I usually come home with a plan for a book. Not always, though. I once came home from a trip with a notebook full of plans for a new novel that I promptly discarded. It wasn't the Mediterranean's fault; the outline just didn't work. Even then, I had momentum, and I knew what wouldn't work. That too can be valuable knowledge to have!

Indexing

When my individual notebooks or binders or project notebooks are full, I put a little numbered label on the spine so I can tell in what order they were completed. I don't have a mountain of journals so large I need a ladder to reach the top, as Anaïs Nin had. Nor do I store them in a bank vault, as she did, because I often refer to them to find something I jotted down or want to use.

If you use a single notebook and write on a variety of topics in your notebook, you will want to devise a system that makes it easier to find what you need later. When I fill a notebook, I usually jot inside the front cover a list of the topics or projects I've discussed and the page numbers. Nothing fancy, just a list.

If I have ideas for a project I've been mulling on for some time, they will be scattered throughout a notebook or in several notebooks. In that case, I cull through the notebooks to scout out what I've collected and use a highlighter or colored pen or sticky tabs to mark off those sections; I write the topic at the top of each page so I can find it again quickly.

For a more detailed indexing system, you can number the pages and include a grid on the last page of the book: four blocks across and six down. That gives you one block for each letter of the alphabet, with w/x and y/z sharing the last two blocks. Fill in the topics as you go, with the page number. No need to alphabetize within each block; you'll be able to locate what you need easily enough.

Working out your own system is itself a creative exercise. Enjoy it. Or don't have any system at all. I didn't for many years and didn't miss having one in the least.

Project Boxes or Project Files

In developing projects, your need for idea-capture may expand past a single notebook to include file folders, a box, a cabinet, a shelf—whatever best holds all that you gather. Dancer and choreographer Twyla Tharp used boxes to gather the things that inspired her as she planned a new dance production: CDs, photographs, news articles, notes, toys, a green beret. As she worked on a project, she would return to the box, pull things out, consider why she included them in the first place.

> "This was the first time I kept a notebook for a project (building a home bar). It ended up being a vital part of the process. I took notes on my mentor sessions, kept sketches of the different sections I wanted to construct, noted progress, kept measurements, and used the notebook to keep a 'to-do' list. I also found that as I got deeper into the project, other ideas came to mind that turned out to work very well."
>
> G.J., workshop student

When I practiced law, I kept article files on topics I might need in writing briefs, researching cases, or talking to experts. In that work, things fit into categories. My teaching life usually can be filed neatly, too: ethics cases, employment law cases, ideas for a new class, topics for future research or writing.

But I discovered my fiction writing life couldn't be so easily labeled and filed. I would collect news and magazine articles or photos or notes. Being at times a bit too fussy, I tried to organize them in file folders with labels. But some things wouldn't settle themselves neatly in one file folder; they often fit too many categories to be corralled in such a way. Others were unique: what to do with the engagement photo where the groom-to-be's motorcycle rally T-shirt peeked out beneath his full beard? Or the article on how to tap a telephone line?

When I found I couldn't easily contain the idea stages of my writing life in neat file folders, I started an "incubator file." You might prefer a box, but I use box-bottom hanging files with enclosed gussets so small bits won't fall out. I just throw news clips, photos, forensics articles, legal cases, that quirky engagement announcement, whatever piques my interest, into the file as I acquire it. No labels, no attempts to segregate or organize.

Like a rich primordial ooze, things combine and recombine in there. When I get ready to start a new book or story, I pull out my hanging files—even after many years, there are only three box files, chock full of paper—and thumb through them. I set aside the items that leap out at me. They don't have to be related in any logical fashion; they just interest me enough that I would like to explore them. I comb back through the bits I've selected, I talk to myself on paper about them, about what interests me about the items singly and collectively, about what I'm interested in writing, what would make a good story.

Visual artists, scientists, and others accumulate ideas, too. Da Vinci's notebooks are a teeming repository of all manner of interests. In the same way, those who are starting a business or redecorating a kitchen often collect ideas and resources over time.

☞ USING YOUR BOX. Tristine Rainer, in *The New Diary*, writes: "This process of filing bits and pieces of ideas and gradually developing and elaborating on them could be used effectively by an architect designing an office building or a teacher developing a grant proposal. It can also be a welcome solution to a conflict between practicality and the creative impulse for people whose demanding lives or jobs do not permit much creative expression. You can keep a creative project journal in a kitchen drawer or in an office desk, carry it in the car and record notes for it on a tape recorder. When an inspiration comes you can record it quickly and go on with your other activities. In this way you can develop a cookbook, a novel, or a ship design, a landscape for a Japanese garden, a screenplay or a comic routine while working full-time or taking care of a family."

You may not know why you like that news photo or why the story of a teen's personal struggle or a corporate fraud interests you. Just clip it out, throw it in your box or file. Maybe it won't still interest you in six months. It can hit the recycle bin then. Or it may mysteriously recombine with another item and lead to a startling new business idea or a solution to a problem or a new story. Your collection may highlight a theme that you hadn't realized attracts you.

You may not work in a way that requires a long-term incubator file. A shorter term project file or box works the same way. What if you have a major presentation to give in three months? You've had random ideas floating in your head at odd moments about what you'd like to cover, about an effective technique you saw, about a connection you'd like to make. You've been talking to yourself in your notebook, trying to capture these ideas as they float by. You see a PowerPoint presentation that's particularly well-designed; you throw a copy in your file so you can study the layout. You see a brochure that presents items in a memorable way or a blog about new trends that support the direction you're suggesting. Put it in the box. Let it incubate.

What Can You Expect?

Keeping a notebook helps improve your focus, directs your attention. The more aware and the more disciplined you are, the more you see or hear or understand. You get better at translating ideas into words or pictures or sounds—which are, after all, our chief methods of communicating our ideas to others. You capture your ideas and build on them over time. You rewire your brain or rework your attitudes. Writing, as a tool for cogitating, allows you to translate synapse-fires into expression. Writing forces you to slow down and think deeply.

☛ REASONS FOR KEEPING A NOTEBOOK. Rainer, in *The New Diary*, listed the reasons most frequently mentioned for keeping a notebook or journal:

"A healthy release for feelings and tensions ... a place to advise yourself, clarify your goals, and make decisions ... ... a place to rehearse future behavior ... a technique for focusing your energies on what is immediately important ... a way to organize and expand your time ... a place to find creative solutions to problems ... a memory aid ... ... a guide to finding clarity in the midst of crisis or change ... a device for discovering your path and taking responsibility for the direction of your life ... ...

"A place to develop skills of self-expression ... ... a place to record meaningful insights ... a quiet place to relax and refresh yourself ... a device for freeing your intuition and imagination. ...

"A way to learn to trust life ... ... a workbook for creative writing and drawing ... a safe place to take intellectual and creative risks ... a source book for future projects ... a means of discovering joy within the context of your life."

A notebook also provides a place and a ritual for looking at your goals and your progress. For the purpose of discovering your creative process, I'll again repeat: Use your notebook often—daily, if possible—to firmly establish the routine.

For most of us, ideas come together over time. The more we engage in any process, the better we become—whether the process is hammering nails to make a birdhouse or capturing illusive ideas for a new satellite system design or a novel.

In any creative endeavor, clarity of thinking and clarity of expression are critical. The more you develop your ability to translate the ideas in your head into words or actions, the easier to share your ideas with a broader audience.

Experiments

Each chapter includes experiments to help you explore that step in your creative process. To get ready to capture and cogitate:

❶ Choose a notebook and a pen or pencil. *Tools* are important.

❷ Set aside *time* every day (or, if you must, an afternoon each week or a day each weekend). Identify what you'll give up to make room for this time.

❸ Make a *space* for your creative work. You don't need a fancy study or studio, but you do need space to work and to keep your stuff. Identifying even a small space is an indication of how much you value yourself and your ideas. Something as simple as different colored file folders or a special pen distinguishing your regular work from your creative work can give you enough separation and a sense of substance for your creative work. A certain chair you sit in and your notebook and pen will signal you're on your way.

❹ Start using this time and this space every day, at least until you develop a habit and a rhythm that works for you.

Don't approach your notebook with lofty goals. Just sit down for a few minutes and scribble.

:: Prompts ::

From the following suggestions, pick the ones you want to explore in your notebook. Or ignore these and come up with your own. Just start writing and thinking!

❑ Talk to yourself (in your notebook) about why you picked this book to read. Why do you want to understand creativity and its process? What do you want to *do?* Why? What will be on your "done" list at the end of this month? This year?

- ❏ Talk about what kind of creative exercises you'd like to explore, what you'd like to play with.

- ❏ Draw a picture of your desktop; diagram your study or your ideal study, studio, or individual space; sketch your coffee cup.

- ❏ Copy quotes that inspire you and talk about why.

- ❏ Make lists—lists of things to do, lists of things you have done, things to stop doing.

- ❏ Write about where you'll be and what you'll be doing in a year, in five years, ten years, twenty years, when you're old. (And when will you be "old"?) What will your life look like? What do you hope you've accomplished? Focus on what you consider "small" things as well as the "big somethings" you hope for.

- ❏ How will you know if you are successful, in a project or in your life? How do you measure success? What if the thing you desire most (having children, being a successful filmmaker or singer, writing a bestseller, being awarded a patent) never happens?

- ❏ What is most valuable to you? Who are your heroes? What do you admire about them?

- ❏ What's on your "bucket list"—the things you want to accomplish before you kick the bucket? Write your obituary. Pretend a historian is writing your biography; what evidence could the historian uncover that tells about you and your life?

- ❏ What would you do even if you didn't get paid for it?

- ❏ What was the last creative exercise you engaged in? When was that? In what ways did it work? Not work? What did you learn?

- How can you use skills you've developed in a hobby or other activity in your personal life? How can what you've learned about your creative process help you at work?

- Make lists of favorite books, favorite places you've visited, places you would like to visit, best ghost tours, best hamburgers in town, or whatever you want to explore.

- List 50 uses for an old paperback book. This exercise develops your divergent thinking skills, a measure of your creative flexibility. Periodically try this exercise with other objects—a newspaper, a pencil, or a product your company manufactures. Brainstorm solutions for things that bother you or that don't work well.

- What are you engaged in when you lose track of time? When does that happen? Can you recreate that experience?

- Has someone ever complimented you on doing something and you were surprised because you thought it was easy or that everyone could do it? Why is it easy for you and not for others?

- Even though you are good at it, what would you like to *stop* doing?

- What do you do in your work that others find most helpful or valuable or which helps them avoid some "pain"? What comes easily for you that others are willing to pay you to do?

- If you had only a year to live, what would you do with that time?

- If you didn't have to work for a living, what would you do with your time?

- Have you ever had trouble selling an idea to a boss, family member, or other decision-maker? What would improve your chances of success next time? What did your idea look like from the other person's perspective?

❑ If you were hiring someone to do your job, would you hire yourself? What do you bring to the task that is valuable, unique, worth your salary? What skills do you need to strengthen or what do you need to improve?

❑ "I wish I had a picture…." Think of the occasions in your life you wish you had on film, either as a photograph or a movie. Describe these scenes in words. Consider turning these into a "photo" album of word pictures.

❑ For a week, write down every idea you have about a project. At the end of the week, review them. Had you forgotten some of your ideas? Which ones still seem workable or interesting? What can you build on or combine? Continue using this process until you've fully developed the project or idea.

Chapter 4
Ramble

> "A creative thinker is alive only so long as he grows; you have to keep learning new things to understand the old. You don't really have to change fields—but you must stoke the furnace, branch out, make a strenuous effort to keep from being locked in."
>
> Paul Halmos, mathematician

Few have rivaled Charles Dickens as either a writer or a walker. "If I could not walk far and fast," he said, "I think I should just explode and perish." Biographers say his intimate acquaintance with places and people, cutting across social strata, fed the rich cultural portrait of England he drew and the characters he created. His awareness of London and environs in all their glory and bleakness came first-hand from his walks. He would often walk until he broke free of the urban bounds of London; one morning, he left at 2 a.m. to walk the 30 miles from his town house to his country house.

For Dickens' friends, trying to keep up with his four-mile-an-hour pace was a punishing endurance contest. For Dickens, his walks were a pleasant necessity. But Dickens didn't confine his rambling to walks or his life to writing. He also became a businessman and publisher; he became an actor and producer; and he expanded his empire internationally. He didn't confine his rambles to country lanes. And neither should we.

I've heard lots of objections to the notion of rambles—many of them inside my own brain. One objection: *Isn't rambling just an excuse to waste time and not work?*

To some, the suggestion they should ramble around exploring a lot of different things will seem the rankest waste of time. Fine. Complain about it in your notebook, or call the ramble something else, but ramble you must. To build your creative abilities, rambling—whether physical or mental—is crucial.

You may discover something you've never tried before, something you want to investigate in more detail. Or you may just dabble and play for a while, trying lots of things, looking for what you want to pursue. Or you may already know your creative "calling"—you know you want to be a better writer or dancer or inventor or banker. Wherever you start, rambling is essential.

Rambling should be playful. Recognizing that "play" can be work, though, is difficult for some people—mostly for people who haven't watched small children at play and have forgotten how hard kids work at playing.

An executive at Muzak, the world's leading provider of branded music, messaging, and video content, told me a financial analyst complained about a co-worker whose desk he'd passed. "The guy had ear buds in, with his sneakers propped up on his desk, listening to music. You call that work?" *Harrumph.*

To the analyst who spends his days hunched over columns of numbers, ear buds and toe-tapping don't look hard, said the executive. Trying to find music that describes how a women's retail store "sounds" doesn't look like work in the same way mopping the floor or posting account reconciliations does. But any creative process requires discipline and hard work, even when it looks like goofing off.

> "Play is an essential part of the method for first-rate creative people. For repeated creativity, we need a balance—sometimes working very hard and sometimes playing, sometimes drawing on our experience and sometimes putting it aside. We adjust the rhythm to serve both the routine and the creative challenges of our work."
>
> Mark Stefik and Barbara Stefik, researchers

Rambling is simply an extension of that challenging playground.

Another objection to rambles: *Shouldn't you focus your rambles on something clearly related to what you're working on?* If you're a writer, why stray off to watch a ballet or draw with sidewalk chalk?

Artists accomplished in one art form find that playing in another discipline gives them new insights into their own discipline.

Rambling far from where you feel comfortable can feed your primary passion, exercise parts of your brain that aren't as fully developed, distract you for a while from too narrow a focus, fill your well of ideas. Rambling is both an important starting point and a source of renewal.

> "Sometimes I have found the stimulation of another discipline helps to make my primary creativity even richer.... The main thing is to never listen when people tell you that you can't do something simply because it is not what you do, or have done. I find that often it is just such a time when venturing to learn something new is most important."
>
> Judy Collins, singer/songwriter

If you already have a focus for your creative life—you are a writer or dancer or gardener—rambles can enrich that focus. If you don't have a single focus, rambling may help you decide where to concentrate. Ideally, though, a ramble should have no explicit purpose.

What's a Ramble?

What do you do when you are rambling? Try things you haven't tried before or done in a while. A ramble can be morning pages or chatting to yourself in your notebook with no purpose other than sweeping clutter from the doorstep of your mind. Take a painting class or salsa dance lessons though you think you'll look like a frog in a blender. Visit a modern art museum or attend an opera even though you don't understand what you're experiencing. Take a walk. Practice solving math problems or plan a birthday party.

The more you make time for rambling, the more mindful, more aware, more open to new techniques or prompts for solutions you become. Practice makes it a habit—a constantly open door for new ideas.

The creative process starts with rambling, but you should continually *return* to rambling, too—for rest, renewal, new inspiration. The creative process seldom moves along a linear path. "Rambling" is as good a place as any to get comfortable with the peripatetic nature of creativity.

Decide for yourself what form your rambles take, but I suggest you at least try a few that have successfully sparked others' creative acts. Mix up your rambles, and include some you think you might not enjoy.

The best rambles? Those that scare you at least a little.

Take your notebook or a notecard to scribble on. Reflect on what you've experienced, your reactions to it. Record it in words, a sketch, a photograph, an audio recording. You may not look back at it again—or in it may be planted the seed for your next grand idea.

Where to Ramble First?

:: Take a Walk ::

Walking may be the oldest jumpstart for creative thinking, and its effectiveness has been validated by neuroscience research (and Dickens). In his book *Brain Rules,* developmental molecular biologist John Medina explains that both our bodies and our brains are hardwired for physical activity. "From an evolutionary perspective, our brains developed while working out, walking as many as 12 miles a day. The brain still craves that experience, especially in sedentary populations like our own."

While the brain is not a muscle, it operates much like one. "Exercisers outperform couch potatoes in tests that measure long-term memory, reasoning, attention, problem-solving, even so-called fluid intelligence tasks [a measure of creativity]," said Medina. "These tasks test the ability to reason quickly and think abstractly, improvising off previously learned material in order to solve a new problem."

Exercise does not improve all brain function, though: short-term memory and some reaction times appear exempt from the benefit. However, for both evolutionary survival and creativity, improved reasoning, problem-solving, speed, and the application of what you know to new problems are all valuable tools to have in your creative toolbox.

> "Wandering is the best way I know to feed that flame, to answer those questions. Wandering—but with a conscious step, an openness to experience. 'Wandering' may sound aimless, a flotsam and jetsam drift, but it is as purposeful in its way as the migration of monarchs each fall. Like their erratic, drifting flight, it only looks aimless taken a step at a time."
>
> Cathy Johnson, author, artist and naturalist

What prompted the first of our ancestors to move from the trees to the ground and to adapt to walking upright on two feet? Whatever the prompt, walk upright we do. And the very act of walking may have fed the development of our larger-than-the-average-ape brains.

Research also shows that physical activity is one of the best protectors against the damaging effects of aging on the human brain. Anti-aging prescriptions for the brain rest on three legs: [1] social and [2] mental activity (activities that are often a natural part of creative work) combined with [3] moderate physical activity provide a powerful antidote to the loss of mental capacity in aging.

Walking is simple, cheap, requires no training and little equipment, and the number who credit walking as a key part of their creative process is noteworthy. Once you start looking for creative walkers, they're everywhere. Jane Austen was a great walker. Even her characters walked: Elizabeth Bennett in *Pride and Prejudice* shocked her neighbors by showing up after a three-mile walk across the fields, with her petticoats muddied and her "face glowing with all the warmth of exercise."

Writing teacher Brenda Ueland said, "For me, a long five or six mile walk helps. And one must go alone and every day. ...It is at these times I seem to get re-charged." Incidentally, she lived to age 93.

I don't come in from a walk with scenes fully formed. I don't resolve character dilemmas or other writing conundrums. I write best on paper or a keyboard, but I am an inveterate walker. Like Dickens, I've observed things that ended up in stories. Mylar balloons and odd goings-on in a small-town cemetery come to mind...but I digress. I enjoy the change in the weather, the seasons, walking in big cities, on neighborhood streets, in the woods. However, walking on a treadmill while watching TV or plugged into a digital player has never given me increased mindfulness or "new seeing."

Unplug yourself, lace up some decent walking shoes, put on sunscreen or a hat—you don't want to wrinkle—and see what's out there.

:: Go Back to Nature ::

To truly ramble, get yourself outside, away from pavement and people. Even in small towns or rural areas, we too often live lives sheltered from the "real" world. Sit on the edge of a pond. Walk along a dirt road or forest path. Sit on a patch of grass and watch what crawls past.

> "I think too much of town life has done us in; when we don't live...with Nature, we forget how to live at all."
>
> John Galsworthy, writer

In his 2008 Audubon Medal-winning book *Last Child in the Woods*, Richard Louv described the nature-deficit disorder seen in modern American children who have lived truly sheltered lives, removed from the natural world. Even as adults who once played outside, many of us are drawing on a reserve of nature experiences we built as children, when our moms had to call us in as it turned dark. Unfortunately most of us aren't refilling our long-past nature experiences with new ones. No one has to call us back inside; we've already locked ourselves and our children away.

Why is our nature deficit important? Exploring nature, especially for a child, can teach them how to observe and how to take risks in a way that playing a video game cannot. Pulling up a carrot to see if it's "done" yet, studying a bug or an empty turtle shell, coming face to face with the unknown gives a child confidence to face other unknowns.

Not every kid gets to hang off the bow of a boat so he can flip over a dead alligator and check it out. I watched my six-year-old nephew do that one day. Ten years later, he's still not afraid of much.

The natural world is unique and renewing. What can improve on studying the original? Try drawing a leaf. Study a tree. From looking at its branches, what tells you it's round, rather than flat? How would you convey that roundness on a piece of paper? How does the air feel on your skin? Do your steps make noise?

What do you smell? What do you hear? What games did you play outside when you were a kid? When was the last time you went on a picnic?

As part of your rambling, reintroduce yourself to the great outdoors. Slow down and take it in. What does it have to offer?

:: Explore The Arts ::

If I'm a software engineer or a writer, why should I bother rambling off to a museum or a concert? Because those who want to be creative should learn to draw from the wells that other artists use. Painters try jewelry-making or write poetry because artists know the value of playing with someone else's toys, learning to see from a different perspective, leaving their comfort zone. Others grow stale and want to do more than just play with a new form; they seek a completely new creative outlet.

In trying something new, we may be intimidated by our own ignorance. *There be EXPERTS there,* we fear. To overcome our fear of traveling unknown paths, a map may help.

The Muses were, according to dancer Twyla Tharp's description, "those brilliant and charming and vexing daughters of Zeus and Mnemosyne who held sway over the classical arts." The number and responsibilities of the mythic muses changed over time, but their realms are worth exploring because they can provide a map as you set out on a journey to discover the unfamiliar.

The Classic Muses

Muse	Realm
Calliope	Epic poetry
Clio	History
Erato	Lyric and love poetry
Euterpe	Music
Melpomene	Tragedy
Polyhymnia	Choral poetry or sacred song
Terpsichore	Dance
Thalia	Comedy
Urania	Astronomy (the classic science)

As a ramble, pick one or more areas you would like to explore, or pick newer versions of these classical fields. Read some poetry; try writing some. Explore what history has taught us about the field you are exploring. See a play; work backstage at a theater. At first, simply explore the area you choose. Later you can use your notebook to talk to yourself about what these experiences teach you, what you might use to develop new ideas.

Figaro, Picasso, ballet, *David,* and Dickens are still studied and admired and still inspire for a reason. Though we won't like these equally, each touches something basic in us. Creative works that have endured, sometimes for centuries, are worth at least a look, to see what they can teach you about your creative path.

If you do not regularly partake of community arts offerings, pick one thing that appeals to you. Try a Pops concert. No concerts close by? Your library has classical recordings you can check out. Live music is a richer experience, but you can start with recordings. Pretend you paid a lot of money for the tickets and that you can't leave until intermission.

Classical music just won't work for you? Try jazz. Whatever you choose, *listen* to it. Focus. Get lost in the music and the pictures it makes in your head and the emotions it stirs.

Too often we use music as a background for our lives, as if we had a movie score guiding our emotional responses. Good music, with rich harmonies and mature development, deserves to be heard with full attention. Good music deserves to be more than only a background part of your life.

But also listen closely to the background music accompanying your life; what effect is it having?

How do you respond to music? A friend of mine always hears harmonies when he listens to music; he's a singer. I always feel dance steps. Others see visual images, like mini-movies, or feel emotion. What do you see or feel?

Try the same with paintings. Sit in a gallery or museum in front of a work that attracts your attention. Don't say "I like it" or "I don't like it." How does it make you feel? Calm? Disturbed? Uncertain?

You can educate yourself later. For now, enjoy yourself. Opera snobs may not put Gilbert and Sullivan at the top of their list, but that shouldn't keep you from *The Pirates of Penzance* or *The*

Mikado before you try something more serious. Read the artist's notes, the liner copy on the symphony album, the plot summary of the opera, if you wish. Just ramble and observe and enjoy.

☞ JUDGMENT. For a creative journey, is it possible to be too knowledgeable? Graduate students in any field are trained to study experts' opinions and to discern and develop their own opinions. That's part of becoming an expert.

But early or uninformed judgment short-circuits observation. Rambling implies a freedom, an open willingness to take it as it comes.

What of those experiences you don't like—or think you won't like? Not everything will appeal to you, but perhaps you should suspend judgment and push harder in those areas that are more difficult or less appealing for you. Fear and attraction sometimes walk hand in hand.

Branch out. Don't think you like modern art? Go see good art in person. Look at the colors, how the paint is applied. Creativity researchers Jeff Mauzy and Richard Harriman tell of a designer at a web company who was inspired by how the colors pulled her into a Mark Rothko painting; she had been wrestling with a design problem, had taken a break, and rambled to an art museum. That's where she realized the power of color could make her client's website design more engaging.

Notice how the museum or gallery art is displayed. Notice the lighting, the color of the floors. All of these were designed very deliberately. Be mindful of everything.

Write about your experiences in your notebook. Try some sketches of your own—no one will see the results but you. As you continue your rambles, push yourself. Become more sophisticated in your choices.

Reading can also be part of your rambles. When I began working my way (shamefully late in life) through the books of Jane Austen and Charles Dickens, I also read biographies of both writers and watched movie versions (the BBC mini-series) of their novels. To readers, movies are almost never "as good as" the books, but films can be appreciated for their own storytelling power and technique.

Maybe, in your rambling, you will actually ramble—travel can spark creativity. Research the history, culture, and art of a place you are visiting. If you can't travel in person, you can travel by video, book, literature, ancient maps, satellite maps on the internet, whatever your imagination can bring to mind. (See Lavinia Spaulding's book *Writing Away* for creative ways to keep a travel journal.)

Whatever and however you choose to ramble, plot your own journey—metaphorically and really. To commit yourself, write a list of things you would like to do, experiences you would like to gather.

☛ THE ARTIST AND THE MBA. "About a year into my MBA," said artist Lisa Sonora Beam, "I was working on a design project for a client. After working peacefully for a couple of hours on a new concept, I suddenly realized that all the usual stress and anxiety of facing the blank page and having to create on demand was absent. I wasn't questioning my value as a designer or stressing about what the client would think of the work (or me) or how it (or I myself) might not be good enough. I was simply, miraculously, working away without negative comment from my inner critic and without feeling overwhelmed. This was so contrary to my usual experience that it startled me.

"Trying to figure out what had happened, I remembered something from my psychotherapy training in Carl Jung's work. He said that when you strengthen your non-dominant capacities, what you are naturally good at gets stronger. For me, this meant all the math, quantitative analysis, and linear thinking required for my [business school] coursework not only gave me new skills but was also working behind the scenes, strengthening my natural powers of creative intuition and imagination—all things that have come easily and naturally to me. Exercising my non-dominant functions not only helped me do the math—literally—but opened up new worlds of anxiety-free creativity."

Author F. Scott Fitzgerald offered the same advice in a letter to a friend at school: "I don't want you to give up mathematics next year. I learned about writing from doing something that I didn't have any taste for."

"The faculty of creating is never given to us all by itself. It always goes hand in hand with the gift of observation. And the true creator may be recognized by his ability always to find about him, in the commonest and humblest thing, items worthy of note."

Igor Stravinsky, composer

Why and How to Ramble

Rambling strengthens important creative skills: awareness, observation, problem-solving, risk-taking. But it also raises questions about how to ramble: Alone? With others? With a purpose in mind or just for fun? Some of it, you'll have to make up as you go along, but some guidelines might be helpful.

:: Practice Mindfulness ::

To be creative, you must learn to focus, to pay attention, to be mindful of what is around you.

We become consumed with efficiency. We become successful by being able to quickly sort through impressions and make judgments about what is worth keeping, doing, noticing. We are bombarded by stimuli and are rewarded for moving fast. Yet in developing those skills we can lose the ability to really focus. Slowing down and paying attention, though, is one of the first elements in a successful creative process.

☛ PUTTING YOURSELF WHERE YOU CAN SEE. Arnold Hiatt, former chairman of the Stride Rite shoe company (who is fond of making soup in his spare time) was traveling to meet a competitor to talk about buying one of its poor-performing divisions. "When I travel, I look at children's feet, I look at women's feet. But here I was, traveling by [their] corporate jet and limo, and that's how their executives were traveling; they couldn't see what people were wearing."

What does paying attention bring you? Most creatives talk about finding recurring themes in what draws their attention, and those recurring themes are often the patterns from which they create. Artist and professor Anna Held Audette asks, "Do you find your eyes and your attention returning to certain things again and again?… Somewhere among the answers lie the road markers for finding your own expression. You may very well not know for a long time which of these answers are the most significant; however, you can be certain they all point in the right direction."

The ability to *listen* to others, to truly listen. The ability to *see*, to be in the moment. The dividends should be self-evident.

How to gain these skills may not be so evident. Focus and depth aren't valued in an age where tweets have replaced conversations.

Especially in an age of immediacy, the advice of John Ruskin, 19th century English art critic, artist, and writer, may seem old-fashioned. He didn't consider art a frivolity for his students at the Working Men's College. He saw art as a key to observation—a very practical skill. He taught them to see by sending them out with pencils and sketchbooks. His instructions about how to observe were detailed: learn to see by noting the subtle gradations of color that give a ball its form or the shadings in a white bowl that give depth. To learn to draw—and observe—we must recover what Ruskin called "*the innocence of the eye.*"

Our other senses also benefit from practiced observation. Writers who want to master dialogue should sit and listen. Go where you can overhear others talking. Close your eyes. Can you capture the cadence? Where are the speakers from? What do they do for a living? Are they upset, happy, bored? How do you know?

At times, I find it difficult to allow myself time to observe. I feel I should be *doing* something, anything, but we need to give ourselves permission to sit. The ability to observe is not passive or easily acquired. Stanislavski pointed out that developing this ability "calls for a tremendous amount of work, time, desire to succeed, and systematic practice," which is why so few people can truly *observe*.

☞ PAYING ATTENTION. Constantin Stanislavski, the famous method acting coach, encouraged actors to pay attention. "An actor should be observant not only on the stage, but also in real life. He should concentrate with all his being on whatever attracts his attention. He should look at an object not as any absent-minded passerby but with penetration. Otherwise his whole creative method will prove lopsided and bear no relation to life.... Average people have no conception of how to observe the facial expression, the look of the eye, the tone of the voice, in order to comprehend the state of mind of the persons with whom they talk. They can neither grasp the complex truths of life nor listen in a way to understand what they hear. If they could do this, life, for them, would be better and easier, and their creative work immeasurably richer, finer, and deeper."

:: Find Connections ::

The ability to observe what would otherwise be overlooked or ignored can help us connect seemingly unconnected bits. Observation allows us to see connections that others miss. Some of us very deliberately set out to play in areas different from our own, looking for those new connections or the stimulation of new ways of thinking. Others stumble across those connections while simply playing at what interests them.

Some of us don't find connections because we don't want to leave our area of expertise to become mewling newbies. We don't want to step around the podium and take a seat in the audience.

"Communication across disciplines is unusually difficult because our mind is not particularly eager to learn new jargon and techniques, or to admit that we need to do so," said creativity writer James Adams. "We are afraid that our need to learn new information will be interpreted (mistakenly) as a sign of ignorance."

However, finding and appreciating these connections—between one branch of science and another to solve the mystery of DNA, between law and science to craft meaningful public policy, between medicine and politics to solve social problems—are vital to effective creativity.

Research shows that we need to ramble because we need to fill our brains with lots of different stuff. Subconsciously, our brains draw on what we've already experienced when looking for connections and testing options to solve a problem. Better solutions come not from the most brilliant people but from those with the most knowledge and experiences to draw on. Those surprising connections won't appear if you aren't rambling around trying new things.

> "The CREATE! class gave me the opportunity to see people who are creative and try to understand what it would take on my part to be able to accomplish my goals. Obviously my goals are not to be an interior designer, but the skills and processes that they go through are something I'm not exposed to on a daily basis, so listening to a designer let me see how someone who is more artistic looks at things."
>
> R.K., workshop student

Broad or Narrow?

Some of us fall in love early with the field that will be our lifelong passion. Others are peripatetic and perennial wanderers. Even those who fiercely settle on drawing or dance or chemistry early in life can continue to wander, gathering experiences and expertise by visiting others' passions to see what they can borrow and incorporate into their own.

A wide net or a tight focus? Lots of interests or only one? Both have benefits—and limitations.

> "He who does nothing, renders himself incapable of doing anything; but while we are executing any work, we are preparing and qualifying ourselves to undertake another."
> William Hazlitt, essayist

Whatever your path, as long as it balances both play and discipline, it can lead to a productive creative life.

Examples abound of those with varied interests. Among renowned poets, T. S. Eliot was a banker and William Carlos Williams was a medical doctor. Two doctors I know are accomplished pianists, and a third makes elegant teddy bears from recycled fur coats. A chef writes haiku. The poet Wallace Stevens was, in his other life, an insurance executive because he didn't want to worry about money and supporting his family, though he said poetry was what kept him alive. Advertising executive David Ogilvy credits his work ethic and attention to detail with his early job as one of thirty-seven chefs in a famous Parisian restaurant kitchen. Emily Craig was an artist and medical illustrator before she studied at Tennessee's famous Body Farm and became Kentucky's chief forensic anthropologist. Novelist Louis Auchincloss kept working as a New York City lawyer, though he started his own firm so he could work part-time; he needed the structure of his "day job" in order to write. Most find they must strike a balance of this sort—and that the balance itself is important not only in putting food on the table but also in feeding their creative spirit.

For a long time, I couldn't figure out how the pieces of my life fit together. I could see how being a lawyer might help a mystery writer with criminal procedures and plot ideas, but where did teaching or (not very good) painting or photography or music or woodworking or ballroom and clog dancing fit in? Over time, I found that learning new things helped me understand the universality of the method and discipline of the creative process. We each have our own process, but we each craft our process from essentially the same building blocks. And the process itself translates from one discipline to another.

At its most basic, understanding our creative process moves us past our analysis of its components (which is important) and opens up our big-picture skills. Developing our process changes the way we think and how we solve problems. We see past one "*right*" answer to many answers, to connections others have missed. We use more of our brains and abilities in more and different ways.

At times, I've paid bills as a musician and as a writer. In other artistic areas, such as dance or woodworking, I'll remain the eternal amateur. In the future, I'd love to try my hand again at painting, though I am the rankest novice. However, as much as I enjoy each of these interests, I knew I needed to put those interests on the shelf in order to focus on my writing, the one thing I wanted to pursue most intently.

Over time, our focus and the connections we make will change, but I've seen, slowly, how the separate pieces fit together. My interests form an integrated whole, pieced together from bits I didn't plan but was instead drawn to. My problem-solving approaches have broadened. When I have gotten glimpses about how my odd bits of talent or my scattered experiences and random interests fit together, it has been a delight-filled glimpse at a complex and enchanting puzzle. The glimpses have left me determined to continue to grow—and to trust that it works toward an integrated whole.

In traveling along your creative path, pay attention to what attracts you. Those of you who know what single interest consumes you are far down the path already—already identifying yourself and seen by others as an "artist" or expert or professional. For many of us, though, we have too many interests. In that case, we may need to discipline our choices, realizing we can't pursue everything.

☛ Too Much?

For a time, you may find yourself suspended in a perpetual state of play, without much focus. You want to try lots of different things. You leap from one interest to another with the lively abandon of a waterbug in a lily pond. Don't take yourself too seriously. Be content at first to explore, to play, to see what works best for you. But don't get so lost in exploring and playing that you fail to produce anything.

A word of warning: even accomplished artists find that rambling can become a trap for those afraid to commit to a project. It is, after all, easier to play than to work.

You may find yourself with an odd mish-mash of intense passion, too many interests, or even too few. You'll better understand the mess of it all once you understand the nature of creativity and your response to it. Those who have not yet mastered the discipline of the creative process may find themselves scattered and uncertain: "I have too many interests." "I don't do anything well enough." "I don't know where to get started." "I never seem to finish."

Balance, though, is a key concept in creativity we return to again and again. We must be willing to play, but we must also have the discipline to settle in and work. We must focus intently but also be open to whatever wanders in and attracts our attention. We must be willing to look silly and to accept failure. The reason the whole affair looks like a mish-mash is that we are each at different stages in our creative maturity and, at the same time, at different stages in a particular creative project. We have to see a map of the whole road before the spot on which we are standing makes much sense.

Alone or Together?

One of the aims in developing your creative process, as creativity expert Rollo May pointed out, should be developing your "capacity for the *constructive use of solitude*. It requires," he said, "that we be able to retire from a world that is 'too much with us,' that we be able to be quiet, that we let the solitude work for us and in us."

May is right. Some of us fear being alone, but our creativity depends on becoming comfortable with aloneness. We must learn how to preserve our solitude. It may be difficult to find time to do our work or to make our art. We must learn to make the time for aloneness and to use that time effectively.

> "It is a characteristic of our time that many people are afraid of solitude: to be alone is a sign one is a social failure, for no one would be alone if he or she could help it."
>
> Rollo May, creativity expert

Books on how to be creative often encourage us to play and explore on our own, without spouse or children. This is especially important for those who have lost their individual identity to their roles as spouses, parents, and employees and need to rediscover their own creative needs and abilities. That can be difficult, but it is important, so in cases where family members or friends will ridicule or eclipse your creative efforts, you should go play by yourself.

However, in the rambling stage, you needn't always play by yourself. One of the best ways to see things with new eyes, to remember how to play, is in the company of a child. My nephews are not wide-eyed, wide-open toddlers any more, but they still make me laugh and still teach me things.

If you and your spouse can enjoy sharing an experience, do it together. Each of you may be going on the hike or taking the class looking for different things, but building your relationship and building your creative capabilities need not be mutually exclusive.

Eventually, though, you must find time to be alone, to write in your notebook, to sit and watch clouds and mull on whatever comes to mind. That seemingly undirected freedom to explore is an important component in the creative process, so take time to understand how it works for you. Even small amounts of time on a regular basis yield dividends.

As writer teacher Brenda Ueland described it, we need to "noodle around," but we don't. "And that is why these smart, energetic, do-it-now people so often say, 'I am not creative.' ... *This quiet looking and thinking is the imagination; it is letting in ideas.* Willing is doing something you know already, something you have been told by someone else; there is not new imaginative understanding in it. And presently your soul gets frightfully sterile and dry because you are so quick, snappy and efficient, about doing one thing after another that you have not time for your own ideas to come in and develop and gently shine."

So do whatever helps you noodle around and see things with new eyes, whatever provides time for your own ideas to come in and gently shine. Find the balance between exploring alone and with others and what works best for you at different times in your life and in your creative process.

Amateur or Expert?

Part of any creative life is lived as an amateur. Successful creatives maintain a childlike openness, a willingness to learn, a delight in play.

Rambling or play has a part in developing both your individual creative projects *and* your creative life. Rambling is a stage that gets you started *and* one you return to, where you try new things, explore new territory. You are not looking for anything in particular; you are open to everything.

> "Great artists are actually the greatest amateurs—from the Latin verb amare, to love."
>
> Julia Cameron, writing coach

As you ramble, if you find a new idea or concept, the hint of a solution, great. But that is not your quest at this point. Go in search—and take what comes.

In the area where you will concentrate your creative efforts, expertise will be important. You must learn the basics. Your creative work will have a learning curve, but then, what worth pursuing doesn't? Photographers must learn their cameras. Poets must know—and love—words.

However, expertise can get in the way of seeing with new eyes and finding new paths, which is why "ramble" is a separate and early stage in our creative process. "Although some expertise is needed to be creative in any area…too much expertise can interfere with creativity," Robinson and Stern observed. Those with experience "have developed the ability to recognize patterns that novices do not see and have 'scripts' for dealing with the particular problems in their field." On the other hand, though, "the longer a person has success with a particular paradigm, the harder it is to let it go when it no longer applies."

You may not choose to live your entire creative life as an amateur, but the Ramble stage reminds you of the continual need to play. That freshness, that awareness, that continual flow of new experiences is vital. Some of those experiences will be a superficial encounter with an art form or a place. Some will be more in-depth explorations of your area of expertise.

> "Since I started exploring my own process, I am more willing to try new things that I find interesting without worrying about what others think. I am more open to new ideas and other people's creative process, and it is okay to have several different projects going at one time."
>
> B.G., workshop student

Eventually, of course, in your chosen area (or in multiple areas), you will move past the fun of play to a dedicated passion. To see the difference, watch people who are learning how to ice skate, then watch Olympic ice skaters. Better yet, think of a physical skill you have mastered: piano playing or dancing or throwing a football. At first, you concentrated on the basics in a disjointed fashion. My foot goes here, my arm does this. Your movements were more like those of Frankenstein's awakened monster, not like the ideal you hoped to emulate.

Then, one day, at one moment, when you weren't paying attention, you moved from *thinking* to *knowing*, from *analyzing* to *doing*. The swing of the bat or the three-count waltz became yours, not something separate from you.

As surely as a sandlot baseball player has to work his way to the majors, so also we must put in the time and gain the skills necessary to move into the professional ranks—or even those of the accomplished amateur.

> "Moving between fields is the way to be creative. Keep your fingers in a lot of pies. I do it because I'm curious. I'm the only person I know who goes into a poster session [at a scientific meeting] and stops at the first poster I have no idea what it's about. Find the poster you don't know anything about and look at it for a long time, and you might learn something totally different."
>
> Kary Mullis, 1993 Nobel prize in chemistry for inventing PCR to amplify DNA

"Amateur" isn't a derogatory term in the creative realm. Amateurs do some amazing things. An amateur recently used a calculator and information from a website to locate and photograph a tool belt that slipped away from a space-walking astronaut repairing the International Space Station. Author Ernie Zelinski reminds us of others who scored noteworthy accomplishments in fields in which they didn't formally train:

- "The Coca-Cola logo was designed by an accountant with no training in art.

- Samuel Morse, an artist, invented the telegraph.

- Robert Campeau, an eighth-grade dropout, amassed a billion-dollar department store empire.

- The Wright brothers invented the airplane. They were bike mechanics and not aeronautical engineers.

- The ballpoint pen was invented by a sculptor."

However, though their paths might have been unconventional, these noteworthy amateurs were not untrained. I don't know much about quantum physics, but I doubt many of the Nobel Prize winners of the future will come from the ranks of those with no knowledge of Planck's constant and string theory. Just a guess. For the amateur as well as the expert, a revelation is, as Robert Grudin puts it in *The Grace of Great Things*, "impossible without groaning effort, with the painful winning of skill."

So what does this "groaning effort" have to do with your creative process? What do the sandlot baseball player aiming for the big leagues and the do-it-yourself space scientist have in common?

☞ THE WIZARD OF BERKELEY

Edward O. Heinrich, a Berkeley, California chemist in the 1920s, became the stuff detective novels are made of, the American Sherlock Holmes. Disgusted with the charlatans passing themselves off as forensic scientists at the time, he stepped past the bounds of his chemistry lab and educated himself in such diverse fields as handwriting analysis and ballistics.

He was happiest when immersed in an intellectual puzzle. In October 1923, when Train #13 was waylaid and robbed at Tunnel 13 in mountainous Oregon, the investigators brought him just such a puzzle: some stained denim overalls and cloth shoe covers found near the scene.

After studying the two items, he told them to look for a fastidious, left-handed, Caucasian, Pacific Northwestern lumberjack, around twenty years old, 5'10" or shorter, about 165 pounds, with small feet. Wow! A crystal ball?

No. The stains were tar pitch; he judged the suspect's size from the shoe covers and overalls, which had fingernail clippings (pointing to his neatness) and woodchips in the pocket and more wear on the left pocket than the right. A receipt wadded in the bib pocket led to the DeAutremont brothers, one of whom matched the description.

Heinrich's cases make him one of the most remarkable real-life crime-solvers in forensic history—thanks to his astounding attention to detail and the mastery of several scientific fields outside his own.

"Cultivating a beginner's mind is about letting go of grasping and cultivating spaciousness. Too much alertness—trying too hard—leads to agitation. The beginner's mind has a sense of playfulness, lightness, and receptivity." At the same time, the "prepared-mind advice says, Discard your previous experience.... The advice about having a prepared mind works well for routine problems, and the advice about cultivating a beginner's mind is for novel problems."

Barbara Stefik and Mark Stefik, creativity researchers

Those seriously engaged in a creative act love what they do, so they spend time getting good at it. "At times creativity cannot escape from simple hard labor," said researcher Frank Barron. "Deadlines to be met, canvases to be stretched, scales to be learned and repeated endlessly so that our fingers may match our inspiration. The dedication to mastery needs the mastery of practice, and the exhilaration of creativity is sometimes counteracted by drudgery. Yet the drudgery of practice takes on a different light when we see our plodding efforts turn into mastery."

In the rambling stage, it's okay to play when you aren't very good at what you're doing. To develop your creative process, though, you should work toward mastery in at least one area. After you've mastered something, stay focused, don't skitter away and use rambling to avoid the work of creating. At the same time, continue to ramble on occasion. As always, seek *balance*.

Experiments

Set aside some time this week and choose a ramble you'll take. Whether half an hour for a walk or half a day for a museum visit, make a date with yourself. Going forward, put regular dates for rambling into your weekly or monthly calendar.

Choose from the following or compile your own list. If you haven't written down both your plans and the time in which to ramble, you haven't fully committed yourself.

Use your notebook to talk to yourself about what you've seen and done and how it felt.

:: Break a Habit ::

To jumpstart your synapses, try breaking some of your most basic habits. For example, wear your watch on the opposite arm. Which shoe do you put on first every morning? Put the other one on first instead. Cross your arms; which is on top? Now re-cross your arms so the other arm is on top. What else are you used to doing without thinking about it? Breaking your habits and trying something new actually helps rewire your thought processes and add new synapses.

To further awaken your brain, vary your daily routine. Pick up your coffee cup with the hand you don't usually use. Take a new way to or from work.*

:: Watch Movies ::

Choose films that explore where artists got their inspiration and how their ideas developed. Some of my favorites include:

❑ Children's book author Beatrix Potter and her Peter Rabbit in *Miss Potter,* starring Rene Zellweger.

❑ Gilbert and Sullivan and the Japanese Village exhibit in Knightsbridge that might have inspired their comic opera *The Mikado,* in the movie *Topsy Turvy.*

❑ An office worker whose talent is making connections no one else sees in *Working Girl,* starring Melanie Griffith.

❑ A rural South Carolina man who becomes a world-renowned topiary artist in the documentary *A Man Named Pearl.*

:: Listen ::

YouTube offers easy access to classical music (though a good digital recording and good speakers improves the experience). Sit and *listen*. Any rich, interesting music deserves your focus. Here are some suggestions to start:

- ❏ *Ride of the Valkyries,* Wagner
- ❏ *Toccato and Fugue in D Minor,* J. S. Bach
- ❏ *Moonlight Sonata,* Beethoven
- ❏ *New World Symphony,* Dvorak
- ❏ *The Four Seasons,* Vivaldi
- ❏ *Canon in D Major,* Pachelbel

Many of these you have heard as background music in movies. What do you experience when you are focused only on the music? Talk to yourself in your notebook about your response.

:: Read ::

- ❏ At the library, choose five magazines to study. For each, ask yourself how the magazine makes money (who buys advertising space)? Describe its ideal reader; be specific. List five articles this magazine might publish that would appeal to its readers and advertisers.

- ❏ Choose an author you would like to know better. You don't have to be a literature major to go on this ramble. Some of my favorites are William Shakespeare, Charles Dickens, and Jane Austen, but you can choose Stephen King or Sue Grafton or anyone else. Read a biography or articles by or about the writer. Check out his website, if he has one. Rent or borrow from the library a DVD of one of her books or plays. (For

Austen and Dickens, I recommend the BBC versions. I love Dickens' *Bleak House*.) Then read one of the writer's books. Read carefully and pay attention to the language. Why did the writer make those particular plot choices? What would you have changed? In the case of classic books, why is this book or this author still read today?

❏ Gather some magazines, novels, poetry, a Bible or other religion text, or newspapers. Go through them looking for quotations that speak to you in some way. Copy 25 of these quotations in your notebook. Compare these. How are they alike? How are they different? Why do you think you responded to these particular sentences?

❏ Visit your library and thumb through books about a topic you want to explore—landscape design, pottery making, better PowerPoint designs.

:: Cook ::

❏ Watch the movie *Julie and Julia*. Read Julia Child's and Alex Prud'homme's *My Life in France*. Does her passion for cooking make you interested in learning more? Read some of the entries in her *Mastering the Art of French Cooking*.

❏ Visit the cookbook section in your bookstore or library to explore other cookbooks.

❏ Pick a recipe and try it.

:: Draw ::

❏ Buy a good sketch pencil and paper at an art supply store. (Good tools are important.)

❏ As a way to get started, draw two parallel lines about one inch

apart. Within these lines, practice shading in a smooth gradu-
ation, from palest grey to darkest black. Keep practicing until
you learn to use your pencil and can duplicate the delicate
shifts in shading. (See image below.)

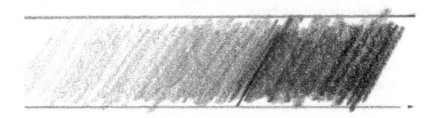

❑ Choose something on your desk or in the room where you
are sitting. Study it carefully. Now draw its outline. Don't look
at your paper as you draw; keep your eye on the object and
trace its outline without looking back and forth from sketch
to object.

❑ For more practice and techniques, try *Drawing on the Right
Side of the Brain* by Betty Edwards or the *So You Thought You
Couldn't Draw* series by Sandra McFall Angelo.

:: Focus ::

❑ Find two of the same natural object, such as an acorn or peb-
ble or leaf, and study them intently. Identify how they differ.

❑ Go outside if possible; if not, sit inside somewhere people are
present. Just sit and observe for ten minutes. What do you see
that you haven't noticed before? What do you hear? Smell?
Feel? Do you overhear or observe something funny? Why is it
funny? After you finish observing, write down what you saw,
heard, felt, or smelled in your notebook. In a couple of weeks,

read your descriptions again. Did the time you spent in close observation make you more aware of your surroundings in the following days? Explore how this ability to focus might help with a problem or issue you are dealing with.

❑ According to creativity researcher Edward de Bono, lateral or *divergent thinking* is a key indicator of creative ability. Those who can generate more ideas and ideas different from those others generate are deemed more creative, based on this measure of both fluency and flexibility of thinking. To strengthen your divergent thinking skills, create a sheet full of circles (like the one below) to fill a sheet of letter-size paper, then work as quickly as possible to turn the circles into pictures of round things. Push past your first thoughts.

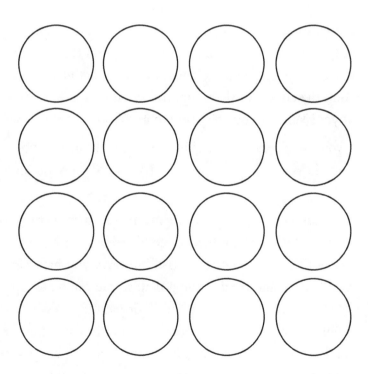

Now go out and spend time noticing round things; then repeat the exercise with another sheet of circles. Have you come up with more and different objects? Does observation enrich the pool of possible ideas from which you can draw when you have something to solve?

Try this exercise with a sheet of squares or triangles rather than circles. Use this whenever you want to limber up your thinking.

❑ For a different divergent thinking exercise, find a common object, such as a newspaper or a metal can or a baseball cap, and think of as many different uses as you can for it, as quickly as you can. Try this with a group to see how others' ideas build on and feed one another.

❑ Go to an art gallery. You don't need an art appreciation course for this experience—though you should take a course if it interests you. Wander around until you find a painting or sculpture that attracts your attention. Spend time looking at it, without judging it. Look at the colors, the thickness of the paint, the curves of the sculpture. What mood does it evoke for you? What is your response to it? Why did it attract you?

In your notebook, list the questions you'd like to ask about the artwork: What's happening? Why? Why did the artist choose this?

The more you know about specific art techniques, the more you can admire what was required to create a piece of art. You may not be a great sketch-artist, but once you have played with shading and tried copying shapes, you can better appreciate the work involved in a sketch or painting to which you respond. For painting or writing or dance or any other form, you don't have to be good at it to appreciate it, but appreciation is enhanced when you have tried to create on your own.

❑ John Ruskin suggested looking at a white bowl, inside and out, to understand how gradations of light and shadow make it look round. Study a white bowl or a clear glass. Can you see the visual clues that tell you about its shape?

:: Make ::

❑ Use old greeting cards or folders or cereal boxes to make mini-journals. Use them to hold your creative plan or list of things to do or as a travel journal or thinking notebook for a specific topic. When you've filled one, you may want to paste or stick it into your regular notebook. Use one to turn your "I wish I had a picture…" stories (page 52) into a handmade book. Or write your own book for someone. I wrote and illustrated *Jack the Munchkin King* to make my nephew Jack king of the land of "it's all stupid" when he decided kindergarten was a waste of his time. For printing set-up instructions, use Google to find "how to print a chapbook" or how to make a notebook.

❑ Using a 5x7 card, create a "calling card" that introduces you to others. Use images or words or three-dimensional items that describe you as you are or would like to be. What would this card tell others about you?

❑ A mandala is, at its essence, a circular design used to represent unity. Using a flower where each petal must balance the one on the opposite side, I've illustrated the balance needed between the elements used in developing our CREATE! process (see the image on the next page). Make an illustration of what you need to develop your creative process—maybe it's a path or a globe or a collage. What does it look like?

Creative Process Mandala

:: Imagine ::

❏ Metaphors and similes are unexpected *connections*. "X is *like* or *as* Y" is a simile. "X is Y" is a metaphor, saying that X has become so identified with Y as to *be* Y. For example, "home is like a heartache" is a simile, indicating that home is similar to a heartache. "Home is heartache" is a metaphor, describing what home *is* or has become.

Complete the following similes, but do not stop with your first thoughts, which will tend to be clichéd and ordinary. Dig for more unpredictable, original, and unusual comparisons. After you finish the first set, do another set of responses that are humorous.

Nervous as _____

Flies like _____

Like moving _____

Easy as _____

Lumpy as _____

Dry as _____

Regular as _____

Crooked as _____

Red as _____

Rich as _____

In your notebook, try more of these. Make this one of your routine brain-stretching exercises. For other examples: *I Never Met A Metaphor I Didn't Like: A Comprehensive Compilation of History's Greatest Analogies, Metaphors, and Similes,* Mandy Grothe (2008); *Metaphors Dictionary,* Elyse Sommer (2001); *Falser Than A Weeping Crocodile and Other Similes,* Elyse Sommer and Mike Sommer (1991).

❏ Identify a persistent, nagging problem at home or work or in your community or organization. Why does it bother you? Put yourself in the position of anyone who may be causing this inconvenience or bother. What is his perspective? What solutions could you propose for fixing it? Don't rely only on your first impressions or ideas; remember, the best ideas come later, after the first rush of ordinary answers. Write about it— over several days, if you like.

:: Design ::

❑ Design your own personal logo or icon. Businesses design combinations of pictures, words, and colors to convey something about who they are and what they do. What would your logo look like? What small graphic depiction could explain who or what you are? Think first about the elements, then combine them.

❑ The things you have in your house are things you enjoy, aren't they? William Morris, a leader of the arts and crafts design movement, said, "If you want a golden rule that will fit everything, this is it: Have nothing in your houses that you don't *know* to be useful or *believe* to be beautiful." Usefulness can have an objective measure; beauty is more subjective, hence his emphasis on *knowing* it to be useful and *believing* it to be beautiful. When was the last time you really noticed the items in your house? Take a blank sheet of paper or card stock (a dark color if possible) and cut a one-inch square in the center. With one eye closed, use this card as a viewfinder. Focus on certain items in your favorite room. What are they? Why do you have them? What do they say about you? Are there things that shouldn't be there? Why do you keep them?

❑ Something in your house frustrates, irritates, or angers you. What is it? Your hall closet? The messy junk drawer in the kitchen? How to manage all the paper that comes into your house? How to divide up the chores equitably? Figure out a way to fix it. If it involves others, how will you sell them on the idea?

❑ Go to a large home improvement store. Wander the aisles studying the items. Even if you don't know what something is used for, what *could* you use it for? Imagine something you'd like to create using items you've found.

❏ Design a bookcase. In an auction catalogue, I saw a photo of a magnificent dollhouse that looked like an elegant two-story French *maison*. While I didn't need a dollhouse, it struck me what a wonderful bookcase it would make. For me, a mystery or haunted house bookcase seemed just the thing to have. I found molding at a home improvement store and windows and doors at a dollhouse store. I added features inside each window that fit my theme. Design your own chair-side bookcase where the shelves face your chair and the back of the bookcase faces outward and becomes an adobe pueblo, perhaps. Or a horse barn. Or a fairy castle. Whatever you desire. What materials would you use to make it?

- Try your hand at designing a toy, a calendar, a greeting card, a new alphabet, a new desk.

- Design your ideal home for you and your family. If money was not a constraint, what would you have in it? How would it function? What spaces would you want or need? What appliances, furnishings, and fixtures would you have? What colors? What would you *not* have? Where would the house be located?

:: Investigate ::

- Using the library, Internet, and other resources, plan a week-long trip, even if you only expect the trip will be an imaginary one. Where will you go? What will you do? Focus on one particular aspect of your destination—architecture, parks, history, hikes, literature, local folklore, crafts—that you want to experience. Be specific about where you will eat, where you will stay, what you will do.

- A travel company featured a garden gnome in its television ads, taking vacations and finding itself in spots that would be difficult or funny for a garden gnome. Pick an object (a favorite doll or stuffed animal, a flashlight, your shoes, or whatever else strikes your fancy) and take it to work with you or take it rambling on a Saturday outing. Photograph it. Where else could it travel? What kind of adventures would it have?

- Study a roadmap or topographical map. Notice names. Find a book or museum display with ancient maps, the kind where "there be monsters here" should appear at the distant edge. Decorate a map with memorabilia of your honeymoon, favorite journey, or trip you'd like to take one day. Draw a map of your creative process—where you've been and where you plan to go.

❑ John Lane wrote a book entitled *Circling Home*. He took a dinner plate and drew a circle on a map around his home in Spartanburg, South Carolina and explored the stories and natural history within that circle. What do you know about the circle around your home? What do you know about your own family stories?

Chapter 5
Engage

> "Creativity doesn't just bring out the best solution.
> It brings out the best in us."
>
> R.B., workshop student

Play is seductive and some people choose to remain in the rambling stage, trying various media, sometimes for their whole lives. However, most of us are interested in taking the next step on the path and *engaging* in a project or a creative life.

What separates rambling from engaging? Rambling sends you far afield to gather experiences, to explore other creative disciplines, to fill your well of ideas and your problem-solving toolbox. Engagement narrows your range so you can focus on a particular project or question.

To engage means to:

- Attract and hold fast
- Occupy the attention or involve
- Bind, as a pledge or a promise

- Enter into conflict with

- Interlock with (as gears)

- Assume an obligation

I especially like "enter into conflict with," because this is where you start wrestling with your ideas, where you decide to get serious about what you're doing. This is where you make a pledge, assume an obligation, choose what will occupy your attention. In your notebook, talk to yourself about what that means to you.

Hacking Around

According to artist Peggy Hadden, it is "important to remember that, as an artist, you won't get better technically by *just thinking* about your work.... [Y]ou'll have to get in there and hack around, getting better technically as you do. That is your responsibility."

You will likely never feel you've gathered enough information or gained enough skill. Nonetheless, you've got to get to work. You've got to start "hacking around" with the material you've gathered, even if you don't feel quite ready or quite expert enough. The only way to get better is to get started. The book or painting you start now won't be the one you will be capable of creating ten years from now. But simply watching the years pass isn't what brings you to that better book or painting or engineering design or *boeuf bourguignon*. It is the work in which you *engage* that brings you to that point.

> "Begin—to begin is half the work, let half still remain; again begin this, and thou wilt have finished."
>
> Marcus Aurelius, emperor

"Engage" represents the "getting started" phase. It is when you plan, outline, visualize. It is when you decide what the work is to be. It may also be when you start hearing a voice whisper: "You're not ready yet" or "What if you haven't picked the right thing to do?" This is where you must move past those voices and commit to be ready and to get busy. This is when you stop wandering around it and start wrestling it to the ground.

Discipline

How do you engage? Simply put, you must settle in to work, which is simple to say but not always easy to do.

> "Getting started is a common difficulty in every type of creative performance. Even people with great potential for creativity experience this difficulty."
>
> Paul Torrance, creativity and education researcher and teacher

How do we overcome this getting-started hard spot? I agree with Twyla Tharp's bluntness in introducing her book, *The Creative Habit*: "I come down on the side of hard work.... Creativity is a habit, and the best creativity is the result of good work habits. That's it in a nutshell."

Creativity requires *discipline,* which, according to Tharp, is the most important skill—the "ur-skill," as she calls it. "Everyone needs it. No explanation required." The engagement stage is where you develop and exercise your discipline. Not that you must give up the sense of play you have developed, but play alone yields little creative output. That is why rambling is only one of several steps in the creative process.

> "There is no instant gratification in learning to hold the guitar, play scales or cope with aching fingers. Frustration and irritation could have been perfect excuses to abandon this endeavor and fall back upon the relaxed and unstructured style that I have become accustomed to. However, I forced myself—based on the recommendation of nearly every creativity author I read and artist presentation we participated in—to carve out time for this practice, push through the frustration and get to the next level."
>
> J.G., workshop student

One of the myths about artists is that they are flighty and undisciplined. That could not be farther from the reality of productive creatives. True, they tend to know the value of play, which may contribute to their flighty, fun-loving reputation, but they also know the value of discipline and hard work. Otherwise, they would never get anything done.

Initially, artists learn to value hard work because the arts have long apprenticeships. Those who survive know how to engage in the work. When they are cut loose from their mentors, teachers, and fellow students, they must either discipline themselves in their work or sink into obscurity.

Mastery

Discipline has another meaning, too: the body of knowledge in a field. Not only must we learn to work hard, but we must also learn from the work of others and how things work in our chosen field.

☛ SATORI. Creativity researcher Paul Torrance referred to the Japanese concept of "satori" to describe the path toward mastery: "To attain expertness in any worthwhile skills, Japanese commonly expect that it will require many years of intensive training and practice. They regard short cuts as harmful.... It requires concentration and absorption to the exclusion of other things. Generally it involves an intensive, long-term, one-on-one relationship to a 'sensei' (teacher). Above all, it requires persistence—hard work, self-discipline, diligence, energy, effort, competence, expertness." This leads to the highest level of expertness, called satori: "a sudden flash of enlightenment."

At first, we learn from the creative work of others. Painters, scientists, chefs, and dancers all study the masters. Writers must read. In Francine Prose's book *Reading Like a Writer,* her message is simply to read slowly, savor the words, study the effect. Or, what Stephen King identifies as the "Great Commandment" for writers, "Read a lot, write a lot." He makes a vivid point that people who don't read can't be writers. I thought that was a statement too obvious to make—until I was approached at book signings by people who had a book to write...but who didn't read. Do people want to be musicians who never listen to music? Or to paint when they don't like art? Or to be chemists when they think laboratories stink? Perhaps. But why?

If you are one of those inexplicable creatures, go ahead with your lopsided plans. For the rest of you, those in love with whatever creative outlet you feel compelled to pursue, you will have learned what makes a good story or chemistry experiment or painting or project; you will appreciate the effects that can be masterfully rendered.

You will also need to educate yourself about how members of your chosen creative community act. One editor told me, "I was always astonished by the number of would-be writers who knew absolutely nothing about the book business or getting an agent or getting published. They complained about how hard it was to be recognized, but they seemed to have no curiosity about the world they claimed they wanted to enter."

Mastering both sides of discipline—your work habits and your chosen field—means committing time, money, and attention.

☛ READING WHILE WRITING. I knew the value of close and constant reading if I wanted to write, but then I encountered an unexpected roadblock. When I began writing mystery fiction in earnest, I found I could no longer read mystery fiction. At all. I could not lose myself in a story. I could no longer become completely immersed in another writer's creation. It was horrible. I was too busy looking for the strings and struts that moved the characters and held the fictional world together. No more devouring books (plural) each week. No more delightful oblivion. I read slowly, laboriously. I had to stop.

Fortunately my years of devouring novels, particularly mysteries, had provided me with the background in the genre, knowledge of writers and their characters, of types and subgenres, of stories, methods, and techniques. I had a rich store from which to draw as my reading shifted to nonfiction.

Nonfiction, I found, also fed my creative writing. I began amassing books and reports on historical crime and forensics cases told by some amazing crime historians, scientists, and storytellers. I read history, science, travel essays. I began to fill in some sad holes in my reading history; during this time I found I could read 19th-century novels while I was writing mysteries, and thus fell madly in love with Charles Dickens and Jane Austen.

I'm not the only writer who has found herself unable to read while writing. I don't know what the equivalent roadblock or "deprivation" is for those in other fields, but one probably exists. Maybe you won't encounter it. Find a way to work around it if you do.

Space and Time

To help establish a habit or discipline, we need a place to work and the proper tools. Artist Peggy Hadden observed that having your work area set up can become "mildly Pavlovian," prompting you to be ready to work as soon as you are in that place just as surely as Pavlov's dogs salivated whenever the dinner bell rang. Setting up a work area need not be complicated, but it is vital. What do you need? For a writer, a notepad and pen or pencil will suffice. A painter or sculptor or woodworker will need more equipment. Gather your tools, but also focus on simplicity.

However, waiting until you have an art studio with the perfect light, a sound studio with the latest equipment, or a writer's retreat with a breathtaking view is not going to make you creative. It's going to make you procrastinate. Quit wasting time, get just what you need, and get to work.

☛ ON STEPHEN KING'S DESK. Few have illustrated the value of simplicity as well as writer Stephen King who, once he became successful, could afford to quit working in the laundry room with his typewriter balanced on a child's desk. When he could afford it, he got what he'd always wanted: a T. rex-sized slab-of-oak desk, as he described it, sitting under a skylight in his large office. Eventually, though, he opted for a desk half that size and turned it to face the wall, tucked under an eave so he could avoid distractions. Remember, you wish to be engaged in your work rather than creating and re-creating your workspace (unless, of course, that is what you've chosen as your creative project!).

As seductive as waiting on the just-right space can be, waiting on the just-right time can be even more seductive. Managing your time will prove more important than having the most expensive tools and the perfect space.

Those with small children (especially single parents) or those who work long, taxing hours or who have little money to spend on supplies or training—all face particular challenges. After I began writing in earnest on my first novel, I was persuaded to take a five-year job that consumed all my mental and physical energy. "Write" was on my to-do list every day, along with "exercise," and both were usually pushed so far down the list they fell off at the end of the day.

I got out of that five-year job, and soon after that my first book was published, but it had taken most of ten years to become publishable. I still worked full-time, just in a job with different demands, but I took a huge pay cut to do it.

Children present different choices than jobs do. Children grow up. That time with them can never be recaptured, so invest yourself in it. But also carve out those bits of time to do what you can to nurture your creative abilities. Include your children when possible. Bargain with other parents to pool childcare duties to give each of you some alone time. If you can afford it, hire someone to help with chores or children for a few precious hours each week.

For me, I determinedly trimmed lots of excess from my life when I got serious about writing—fewer social engagements, less TV watching. I already had no pets or children. At one point, I finally got rid of our one houseplant; I didn't need it chiding me with its droopy leaves.

I know lots of artists who have written books or made other art by snatching small bits of time and quiet. It's not easy to immerse yourself in a large project when you have other demands, but at least make time to keep a notebook or research your discipline or ramble to fill your well of ideas.

Time and space are important, but no one said they had to be boundless or that they were easy to come by. You're creative; you'll figure it out.

On the flip side, business people accustomed to a driven, disciplined demand to produce often talk about having to step back from too much structure. Arts center director Vicky Hardy affirms this: "I have to allow myself free time. And by free time I don't mean an evening at home watching television. I'm talking about totally unstructured, unorganized, undisciplined free time."

For many of us, especially those who work in busy organizations with constant demands on our time, finding space in our schedule to be unscheduled is one of the toughest—and most important—disciplines to develop.

> "'It is only half-an-hour' – 'It is only an afternoon' – 'It is only an evening,' people say to me over and over again; but they don't know that it is impossible to command one's self to any stipulated and set disposal of five minutes—or that **the mere consciousness of an engagement will sometimes worry a whole day.**"
>
> Charles Dickens, writer (emphasis added)

Whatever your circumstances, you need time so you can fully engage. No one will guard your time for you. Write it on your calendar. Commit to it. Make it fit your schedule. This is what prepares you to handle the next steps in the process.

Remember, small increments of time on a daily basis *will* yield creative results. Quit waiting for endless, uninterrupted days—those don't exist for most of us. Take your fifteen minutes or an hour and use it.

Finding Your Rhythm

Rambling is a first step in helping you discover your own interests and how you work best. Is your office or studio always the best place for you to work? What time of day do you work best? Do you perform different types of work better at different times of day? How long can you productively work at a stretch? How does that change over time or between projects? How are unexpected connections discovered?

You are beginning to discover your own interests and rhythms. As I've said, my ideal start to any project is a trip. Something about being away from home, out of my normal routine, seeing new sights and eating new food jump-starts my creative juices. I can't always get my long trips to coincide with the start of a new project, but I try. At whatever stage in a creative project, I try to plan work that is portable and that will take advantage of the normal cycles of my work life and my creative impulses.

Of course, you can't tell your boss you've booked a long flight and a Mediterranean cruise in order to prepare your next client presentation. Don't get lost in that fantasy. You will find your own good work times, places, and habits.

From talking to other writers, I know not everyone works well away from home, which is why you must find what works for you. Whether it works for someone else doesn't matter. We each have different rhythms, and these vary over the stages of our lives. Anne Rice talked about how she wrote her best-selling vampire novels at night. Later, as the subject matter of her books changed, she also found her work habits changing; she began to write during the day.

As psychology researcher Frank Barron and his colleagues observed, "Creativity is a gift, some way, but not a gift that survives without practice."

At first, you will stumble through, experimenting with different options. No project is the same as another, in part because we are always seeking new challenges and ways to stretch ourselves. Awareness of what prompts your best work will help you miss fewer opportunities and catch the wave more predictably.

Find what prompts consistent work habits for you—promise yourself a reward, set goals, do whatever works. Talk to most productive creatives, whatever their field, and you will find they have reliable tricks they use to get the work done—and that they also must sometimes vary their routine.

One of my favorite reminders of the difference between those who find their rhythm, who gain mastery, who become accomplished, and those who just say they want to is a question asked by Nancy Pickard (one of my favorite fiction writers) and Lynn Lott in their book *Seven Steps on the Writer's Path*: "Does the tongue in your shoes call the one in your mouth a liar?" You *say* you want to develop your creative process, but that's not the direction your shoes are facing. Those aren't the steps you are taking. You can develop the habits that can carry you along your creative path, if only you will point your shoes in the right direction and get moving.

Where Do You Get Your Ideas?

One of the questions writers—and I'm sure other artists—are frequently asked is: Where do you get your ideas? One of the most famous answers to that question (and an often-misquoted one) came when a student asked Nobel laureate Dr. Linus Pauling, "How do you manage to have so many good ideas?" His answer: "Oh, I just have lots of ideas, and throw away the bad ones." Learning what to throw away, of course, comes from experience.

My answer to the "whence come ideas" question is that I *look* for ideas. Your notebook and your rambles should have already begun to make this plain to you: Ideas are everywhere—the secret is to see them, or hear or feel or taste them. To be aware and mindful is the key to new ideas. To capture them is the key to being able to use those ideas.

Many of us assume that artists receive *inspiration,* which means literally "breathing in" an idea, which leads to the belief that inspiration is a mystical gift given to only a select few. These chosen ones create easily, without effort, blessed with powers beyond those of mere mortals, right? Wrong. Those experienced at using their creative process snort with derision at the thought of an effortless gift.

The idea of being "inspired" makes it sound so easy and convenient. After all, if I haven't "breathed in" something, I must not be intended to create, right? Reality is not so simple. Artists, even those who acknowledge inspiration or divine intervention in their creative process, are not passive vehicles. "Inspiration tends to visit people who renew contact with the major challenges of some ongoing project every day and who set no time limit on their involvement," said philosopher Robert Grudin.

☞ THE CHALLENGE TO CREATE. Mary Shelley's account of the birth of Frankenstein and his monster is a glimpse inside the process, evidence that solutions don't effortlessly surface unbidden from a well of genius. Engaging with your material may involve a struggle.

In 1816, Mary Shelley spent a damp summer holiday in Switzerland with her husband, poet Percy Bysshe Shelley; their neighbors included Lord Byron. One evening, after reading aloud from a book of ghost stories,

Lord Byron challenged everyone to come up with a ghost story. Mary Shelley struggled unsuccessfully for several days, frustrated she had no idea for a story.

"Everything must have a beginning..." she said, "and that beginning must be linked to something that went before.... Invention, it must be humbly admitted, does not consist in creating out of void, but out of chaos; the materials must, in the first place, be afforded: it can give form to dark, shapeless substances but cannot bring into being the substance itself."

A conversation during the house party about the nature of life and the current scientific debates on whether galvanism [use of an electric current] could some day reanimate a corpse sent her to bed one night into a terrifying waking dream about creating a monster. She then wrote what she saw in that dream. Her husband encouraged her to expand it into a book—the continually popular *Frankenstein*. Without the challenge to create, the raw materials "gathered" during that house party, and her intense effort to come up with a story, would the monster have been born?

Comic genius Charlie Chaplin, in talking about his creative process, said, "Over the years I have discovered that ideas come through an intense desire for them; continually desiring, the mind becomes a watch-tower on the look-out for incidents that may excite the imagination—music, a sunset, may give image to an idea. How does one get ideas? By sheer perseverance to the point of madness. One must have a capacity to suffer anguish and sustain enthusiasm over a long period of time. Perhaps it's easier for some people than others, but I doubt it."

Cathy Pickens

Poet Amy Lowell describes the hard work necessary between the initial "inspiration" and the end result: "It would seem that a scientific definition of a poet might put it something like this: a man of extraordinarily sensitive and active subconscious personality, fed by, and feeding, a non-resistant consciousness. A common phrase among poets is, 'It came to me.' So hackneyed has this become that one learns to suppress the expression with care, but really it is the best description I know of the conscious arrival of a poem.

"Some poets speak of hearing a voice speaking to them, and say that they write almost to dictation. I do not know whether my early scientific training is responsible for my using a less picturesque vocabulary, or whether their process really differs from mine. I do not hear a voice, but I do hear words pronounced, only the pronouncing is toneless. The words seem to be pronounced in my head, but with nobody speaking them. ...The subconscious is, however, a most temperamental ally. Often he will strike work at some critical point and not another word is to be got out of him. Here is where the conscious training of the poet comes in, for he must fill in what the unconscious has left, and fill it in as much in the key of the rest as possible."

In other words, while some ideas may be "breathed in," productive creatives also discipline their work habits to carry them through the less-than-easy stretches.

What Do Ideas Look Like?

How does someone "see" an idea? That depends on the area in which you are working but, more important, on the way your brain gathers and organizes information. Many writers say they see scenes and hear dialogue, almost as if the characters stood in front of them acting their parts in a movie or play. Charles Dickens would startle his children by making faces in front of a mirror or reciting dialogue aloud in his study.

Regardless of the field in which they work, many report they need paper and pen or computer or sketchpad or some other way to capture the thoughts bouncing around in their brains (which is precisely why you are keeping a notebook). They need to grab and drag out ideas that seem only partially formed before they can "see" them.

I seldom plan my writing in my head, without pen and paper. Poet Amy Lowell would agree: "I seldom compose in my head," she said. "The first thing I do when I am conscious of the coming of a poem is to seek paper and pencil. It seems as though the simple act of gazing at a piece of blank paper hypnotized me into an awareness of the subconscious. For the same reason, I seldom correct poems while walking or driving; I find that the concentration needed for this is in the nature of a trance (although that is too exaggerated a word for it), and must not be broken into by considerations of where I am going or what station I am to get out at."

Some, though, can conceive of an idea as a complete whole. Anecdotal evidence suggests this ability is rare, but it crosses many creative disciplines. Mozart allegedly conceived entire musical works in his head while walking; that story, though, is based on a forged letter. His notes show he rewrote and polished extensively, so perfection did not leap full-blown as he strolled Salzburg.

Charles Steinmetz, a respected inventor in the field of electric distribution, was a renowned visualizer. In 1894, two engineers at General Electric approached him with a problem they'd been trying to resolve: In drilling a two-inch hole to cut a two-inch rod in half, how much of the expensive metal would be lost? Rather than sketch and calculate, Steinmetz reportedly puffed his cigar and said, "5.33 cubic inches." He had been able to visualize the lozenge-shaped plug that would be removed and calculate its volume in his head.

For some, ideas must be teased—or forced—out to be explored. Thomas Edison, who was awarded 1,093 U.S. patents (more than anyone in history), would snooze in a chair holding two steel balls in his hands with metal pie pans on the floor on either side of his chair. As he drifted off, thinking about a particular problem, his hands would relax and the balls would clatter into the pans, waking him up. He would jot in one of his notebooks whatever was in his mind at that moment. He wrote millions of pages of sketches, notes, and observations on wide-ranging topics, evidence of a truly prolific creative mind.

Some ideas develop slowly and require lengthy incubation periods. Beethoven recorded his ideas in notebooks. Over time, some ideas would be transferred from one notebook to another, with additions and transformations, until each had matured enough to be used in a finished composition. The process sometimes took years from inspiration to finished piece. Beethoven's notebooks illustrate that, even for geniuses, the initial idea may be a long way from perfection. "Often his first ideas," said poet Stephen Spender, "were of a clumsiness which makes scholars marvel how he could, at the end, have developed from them such miraculous results."

As these examples illustrate, initial ideas are generated by mindful focus, by looking for ideas, by capturing them, and by continuing to work with and explore them. We must be on the lookout for ideas and wrestle them into something we can use.

Wrestling With Questions

How do *your* ideas come? How do you invite and encourage them? In what "language" do they express themselves to you? Do your ideas appear as words? Pictures or diagrams or charts? In mathematical formulas? Recognizing that ideas can be expressed and developed in different mediums opens up possibilities.

For me, ideas start as questions. When I begin a new fiction-writing project, I ask questions. What interests me? For months or sometimes years before I begin a novel, I have gathered stray bits that attract my interest. When I'm ready to engage in a project, I pull out my notebooks and my files of news clippings and photos. I select those items or ideas that particularly draw my attention, without regard to why or how they fit together.

For me, a nonfiction project, the design of a workshop, a course outline, or a business plan also begin with questions and intuitive choices. The ideas I have captured and the information collected will be narrower, more confined than what I gather for a fiction project; perhaps that narrower focus befits reality as opposed to stuff I make up. Still, I continually ask questions. What does the audience need to leave with? Where are they beginning? What do they already know? What else do I need to know?

I also ask questions that deliberately seek *connections* between what interests me in my personal life and what challenges me in my work. *Integration* can spur your creative thinking, especially if you are developing wide-ranging interests (which is why you go rambling).

☞ For my undergraduate students, I once designed a research exercise they had to solve like a murder mystery. Surprisingly, the genesis of that idea didn't come from my love of mysteries but from a high school math conference I attended on a lark with a friend, where a teacher talked about turning math problems into a game.

Thinking through a half-day workshop takes a different path than putting together a 300-page novel. But the rudiments are the same. I have pen and paper at hand, and I talk to myself. In my mind, when I think of "engaging" with my material, I see it as "wrestling it to the ground." I use the same work techniques whether I'm in the planning stages or actually writing the book or engaged in a project.

Intuition

Much of what we know is invisible to us. Our brains process information in ways we don't fully understand, store it in places we may not consciously access. However, the more you engage with your work, the more you learn to trust your intuition.

Intuition is not some spooky, other-worldly crystal ball event. Intuition isn't wishing for something, hoping it will come to light. Studies by psychologists, such as Gerd Gigerenzer at the Max Planck Institute, indicate that intuition is built on close observation and experience, not on some gift only rarely given. In other words, your observation and experience can help you know what to choose and what to avoid. To use your experience, you must pay attention—and have the courage to listen to yourself.

> "A lot of scientists wouldn't agree with me about the creative aspect of science. They think it's a lot of facts—but Einstein felt it was mostly intuition."
> Louise Emmons, rainforest biologist

As undefined or indistinct as it may seem, your intuition has been educated by your cogitating, your rambling, your mentors, and your mastery. Go with it. Learn to listen to your instinct and trust it to help you decide what ideas to pursue and what to discard. The more you trust your creative intuition, the better your judgment will be about the right choice or right direction. Intuition isn't flaky nonsense. It's the coming together of all the work you've done to bring you to this point. Trust it.

Voice or Style

As a would-be writer, I attended innumerable workshops to learn the craft and business of writing. We anxious fledglings would ask the expert editors and agents, "What are you looking for?" We hoped to hear, "Your book." Of course, that's never what the all-seeing, all-powerful agent or editor said, ever. The answer was always the same: "I'm looking for a fresh voice."

"What does that mean?" we fledglings wondered, but dared not ask. Not knowing surely meant we didn't have it, whatever the Holy Grail of a "fresh voice" was.

Over time spent reading with the intensity of a writer, I began to recognize what voice is: that unique way each artist expresses herself. As a reader, you know it as soon as you start reading. If you watch movies with a critical eye, you can see the different vision directors bring to their work.

Eventually, through much writing, I found my voice, by the only path the agents and editors and other writers had recommended: in the act of writing, lots of writing. I developed a comfort with putting scenes that played out in my head on paper, with hearing characters talk and capturing their story.

I also learned no shortcut exists to the confidence that you can use your own words to tell your story. I kept reminding myself that mystery writer John D. MacDonald said a writer's apprenticeship wasn't done until a million words were written. That's a lot of words (and about 4,000 pages).

A fresh voice means trusting what you know that others don't. I haven't had to feed children three meals a day; I've never lived in a high-rise apartment building. But those are ordinary experiences for lots of people—and maybe the experiences from which you can develop your unique voice and tell your stories.

Writers aren't the only ones interested in finding their voice. As visual artist Anna Held Audette wrote, "The individuality of your artistic voice takes a while to mature, but be reassured, it's there."

So how do you develop your voice or style?

One well-kept secret, in discussions about creativity, is that nothing is really new. "All creative individuals," observed writer Paul Johnson, "build on the works of their predecessors." More experienced creators and artists recognize they have learned from, built upon, even borrowed from others.

Dancer Martha Graham, in her *Notebooks,* unabashedly said, "I am a thief—and I am not ashamed. I steal from the best wherever it happens to me." Of course she didn't mean she was a plagiarist. She was acknowledging the debt all of us owe to others, those in our field and those in very different fields.

Unfortunately the secret of learning from others, of trying others' styles, isn't always revealed to us as fledglings. True, I knew Shakespeare borrowed plots from older histories, but no one told me how often all writers borrow plots and characters from real life. In the act of writing, what is borrowed should be transformed into a new creation, but every pearl begins as a grain of sand.

This borrowing doesn't apply only to writers; all of us learn from others. This debt to those who have gone before should be openly acknowledged, especially so those just discovering their creative process will understand its influence. It took me years to realize that the best crime novelists borrow extensively from real life and, at the same time, operate within the "who-dunnit" structure their readers expect. The most original novelists translate reality into truth, something deeper and more applicable to life than any number of real crime cases could be. The best take something that happened to someone else and transform it into something that affects each of us, thanks to their story's unique voice.

☞ We all must learn our field and should learn from the best, but we can also learn from the worst. Who knows how many writing careers have begun with the sound of a book flung across the room in disgust and the exclamation, "I could write something better than that!" As my grandfather was fond of saying, "No life [or, in this case, book or painting or crocheted tea cozy] is ever truly wasted. It can always be used as a bad example."

This borrowing isn't limited to writers. "Students are sometimes told, in the first art courses, that they shouldn't copy, because it will prevent them from being original," said artist Anna Held Audette. "This is poor advice, based on the false assumption that imitation stunts creativity. In actual fact, imitation may be a significant part of the quest to discover your own voice, and dismissing this activity could deprive you of a surprisingly valuable experience."

Few who work in business or technical fields talk about finding their "voice." Just because they don't use the term, though, doesn't mean it's not part of their creative process. Voice, in part, is seeing the connections your brain is offering you, being aware of what's in front of you, what's possible. Voice is the ability to capture that for yourself, so you can more fully develop it *in your own way.*

Voice is also the ability to share that idea with others in language—words, pictures, formulas, sounds—that will speak persuasively to them.

Those in business and technical areas as well as in the arts must learn to express ideas in ways decision-makers, funding sources, or customers will understand. This requires political savvy, the ability to sell ideas even when those ideas may go against the traditional wisdom of the organization. Great ideas don't passively attract support like iron filings to a magnet. Support must be earned, for even the most compelling new ideas.

A less obvious application of the need to find a voice involves the ability to express the idea *for yourself.* This expression must come before there can be a fully formed idea to be "sold" to others. In any collaboration, the ability to articulate an idea sparks the shared efforts that drive complex projects, whether staging a play, launching a satellite, or teaching a pottery class.

After all, according to Newton's First Law of Motion, things at rest tend to stay at rest. Why should someone try something new just because you suggested it? Why should someone give up something that's working fine in order to try what might be better—or might not? What prompts others is often a compelling voice, a unique-to-you way of seeing something, approaching it, resolving it, expressing it, or selling it to others.

The Voice of Doom

Up until this point, you have been wandering about, looking at things, scribbling in a notebook, being observant, sharpening your intuition, finding your voice, trying to remind yourself—or convince yourself—that you are, after all, creative. Maybe you are even starting to take yourself seriously. "Yes!" you say, "I AM creative!"

But now grim reality sets in. At the very moment you engage in the work, as if Pandora's box had tipped its contents across your workspace, you are beset by demons and doubts such as you have never before faced.

Overly dramatic? Perhaps. But most of us, at some point, wrestle with the specters of fear and doubt. Maybe these have not set upon you yet, but that doesn't mean you will be immune. (Might as well lay in some stores of demon-repellent, just in case.)

Stare it in the face. Of what are you really afraid? Few have given a more succinct list of our fears and how they dry up our creative impulse than writer Brenda Ueland: "Criticism, self-doubt, nervous fear which expresses itself in merely external action like running up and down stairs and scratching items off lists and thinking you are being efficient; by anxiety about making a living, by fear of not excelling." The portrait she sketches looks painfully familiar to me, especially the running about looking busy, when I'm really just running away from the work.

Self-doubt and self-criticism spark fear. Another thing most of us fear is what others will think. Ueland also addresses that head on by identifying it as an unbecoming part of our culture: "Sometimes I think of life as a process where everybody is discouraging and taking everybody else down a peg or two. One of the most common discouragements is that American pastime known as 'kidding'—with the result that everyone is ashamed and hangdog about showing the slightest enthusiasm or passion or sincere feeling about anything."

For others, it may be a critical parent's voice from our past or a spouse who is jealous of the time our new pursuits are taking. Whether the voice is our own or someone else's, we hear plenty of doom, plenty that makes us afraid.

> "What is it that we love to do, that brings both satisfaction and challenge? Where do we find our greatest enthusiasms and our deepest fears? Often, what we want the most is what we fear the most."
>
> David Ulrich, photographer

So, what am I *really* afraid of?

That it won't be good enough to suit me or someone else. That I can't do it. That it will never meet the ideal image in my head.

Guess what. Those fears *all* come true! It *won't* be good enough. I *can't* do it as well as I want to. It *doesn't* please everyone, least of all me. Nowhere on that list does it say, "If I fail, someone will kill me and let birds pick my bones clean." None of your creative failures will be *that* bad. All the other failures, you and I both can survive. In fact, failures can actually help us, in strange and unforeseen ways, to do better work.

I found it reassuring to realize that everyone wrestles with fear. If you don't believe me, here is a sampling of my favorites among artists' nods to fear:

- "If I wait to be assured I'm right before I speak, I would be sending little cryptic messages on the Ouija board, complaints from the other side." ~Audre Lorde, poet and activist
- "You may be disappointed if you fail, but you are doomed if you don't try." ~Beverly Sills, opera singer
- "To fear is one thing. To let fear grab you by the tail and swing you around is another." ~Katherine Paterson, children's book author

That successful artists acknowledge fear proves (1) it is real, and (2) successful creatives don't let it stop them.

Engagement is about holding fast, accepting the obligation, settling in to the work, learning to motivate yourself.

You must also learn how to suspend judgment, to set aside or work around your internal editor or critic or your fear of failure. After all, creating and critiquing are two *very* different steps in the creative process. So why let fear stop you before you even get started? Worry later about fixing what didn't work or getting better at what you want to do. For now, dive in, get busy, *engage*.

Cathy Pickens

Experiments

Are you having trouble deciding what to *engage* in? This can be the fault of too little exploration or, on the other extreme, too many passions. Continue to talk to yourself in your notebook and to explore until you begin to see connections. Give your intuition a test flight by listening to what those connections are telling you.

❏ Depending on what you are engaging in, this is the time to gather your tools and build your nest.

   If you are working on a single, targeted question—say, how to position a new product or how to make your front porch more inviting—you will spend less time "setting up" than if you are fitting out your woodworking shop or starting on a novel.

   In any event, think through what you need:

   * Workspace
   * Time
   * Tools and materials
   * Advice, mentoring, or support

❏ To further narrow your focus or to pull together disparate bits, go through your notebook (or file folder or box or wherever you've gathered what has attracted your interest). Use your notebook to talk about *what* you want to accomplish or solve.

❏ Still can't decide what to work on? Or how to resolve it or make it? Or do you have too many problems or interests you are dancing among? No one said this would be easy. This stage involves some heavy lifting. Commit a certain block of time each day to write about this, or explore it in whatever way works for you. This is where you must wrestle your inspirations or ideas or motives or random intriguing bits to the ground so you can use them. What are the recurring themes in what attracts you or blocks your path? What questions come to mind? About what are you passionate? Explore those paths—and don't accept easy answers.

❑ What scares you? What do you fear? What makes you hesitate to try something? Talk to yourself about that. If you need to, seek the willing ear of a friend or a professional counselor or coach if you can't find your way around a fear blocking your way.

❑ To more deeply engage in a project, make sure you have the skills you need. Some skills you have worked much of your life to acquire, but you may need a refresher course or to add to your toolbox. Find a tutor or take a course. Whatever the field you've chosen to dig into, colleges and local arts organizations offer continuing education or short courses in everything from memoir writing to metal-working, from website design to salsa dancing. Taking a course online or joining a special interest group may start as a ramble—or it may instill the routine you need or give you the extra skills to tackle a problem. No one said the stages couldn't overlap!

Committing your time, money, and focus is an important signal that you are serious about the endeavor you've chosen, that you are *engaged*.

Chapter 6
Act

> "There's no right way to start. Like a beginning diver, you have no choice but to leap in.... It takes an act of courage because the odds don't appear to be in your favor."
>
> Anna Held Audette, artist

As a writer, I'm often asked how long it takes to write a book. I suspect the questioners are those who want to write a book but haven't started, and I suspect novice painters or actors or engineers also want to know how long it takes to accomplish something in their fields.

The most accurate answer? "It takes as long as it takes." The physical act of writing a novel can be done in three to six months (omitting the research and the polishing), but the average for the first-time novelist to write and be published is ten years. That sounds frighteningly long, but any published writer will admit the book that is eventually published changes many times during that apprenticeship; the time is not wasted, it is part of the process.

Questions about how long it takes to create a work or solve a problem miss a key point. The more important question to ask might be, "How long did it take you to get ready to write or paint or compose or invent or make that?"

Though it will likely frighten the faint of resolve, the real answer would be, "Most or all of my life."

> "Mischief may easily be done quickly, but good and beautiful work is generally done slowly."
> John Ruskin, essayist and artist

Take heart. What I mean is, the entirety of a creative life is used in every work. Or should be. Even failures benefit your work. Those who intend to create won't be intimidated by the seemingly insurmountable truth. Those who just want to dream won't be scared off, either—they just won't do anything more than dream.

One of the keys to Thomas Edison's success as an inventor was how he refused to see a failed experiment as a setback. Whatever happened, it became a starting point for a new inquiry. On more than one occasion, extreme heat or cold ruined huge stocks of chemicals in his lab; to him, what could have been disasters were new opportunities to study and document, searching for something that might prove useful.

> "Oftentimes in my personal life, things are moving so quickly that details get washed over. I've learned that final outcomes are necessary, but it's experiencing the journey rather than the destination that is often the key to understanding what and how. I've learned patience and to keep trying until you get it 'right.' During my pottery classes, the clay taught me 'Not so fast, you need to learn to center the clay before you can do the next step' no matter how many times I tried to take a short-cut and work with un-centered clay."
>
> H.S., workshop student

☛ THE FIVE PS

Creativity researcher Mel Rhodes proposed creativity can be viewed as having four elements: the *person,* the *process,* the *product,* and the *press (pressure)* of the environment. Psychologist Dean Keith Simonton added *persuasion,* the act of persuading others to accept and adopt the creative product.

In my experience as a creative person, as an observer of other creative people, and as a student of research on the subject, the most malleable of the Ps is *process.* Each of us has a unique set of talents, abilities, and interests; though the *person* can be developed, we start with some givens. Even the most accomplished artists often feel that what they produce falls short of the marvelous ideal they had in mind when they started on a project, so the *product* is not always predictable. The envionment in which we create (such as a workplace) is often out of our direct control. And while skills and techniques in *persuading* others to see the value of a new idea can be honed, even the most persuasive person with the best idea may face an impenetrable audience.

Even though you don't have complete control over your personal abilities, how your ideas pan out, the environment of creation, or how they will be received by others, you do have control over your own *process*. Developing your unique creative process improves your creative abilities and increases the odds that you and others will be pleased with the *product* of your work. Developing your own process will carry you past the rough patches of doubt or challenge.

An oft-repeated but perhaps apocryphal story tells of a renowned maestro approached by a young violinist who wanted to know if he had what it took to be a great violinist. The violinist began to play what, to another listener in the room, was some of the most moving music he'd ever heard.

As the last strains died out, the violinist turned to the maestro, awaiting his pronouncement. The maestro shook his head. "No, you don't have what it takes." The violinist slumped. Stunned by the great musician's words, he left the room.

"Why did you tell him that?" the maestro's friend asked, shocked. "That was incredible music!"

"Because," the maestro said, "if he has what it takes to succeed, he won't listen to me."

Those who have what it takes don't count days or disappoint-
ments. They just do the work. Artists aim for an always-better
result, but they also learn to trust the process.

Although "Act" is only one part of the process, it is the stage at
which you see how everything works together.

Routine

Most who successfully create will tell you their secret is surprisingly mundane: a *routine*. As boring and uncreative as it may
sound, routine and discipline are the by-words of the productively creative.

> "Routine is the one way in which one
> learns not to waste time."
> May Sarton, writer

You've gathered your materials. You have a place to work.
You've found a compelling idea you want to develop. Now all that
is required is that you show up.

Routine is helpful at this stage because too often we want to
shy away or procrastinate. As a novelist friend of mine observed,
"It's hard to start because you know what you're letting yourself in
for." It will be demanding; it's hard work. But, at the same time, it
is also enjoyable, especially when you are immersed in the project
and "going with the flow." At the end—of a project or of a day's
work—is a pleasantly numb sense of well-being. In my own work,

even when I'm not fully pleased with the product, I can usually be pleased with the effort and what I've learned from it.

> "In terms of getting access to creativity, it's very important for me to clear the deck mentally—to be able to direct energy toward just the problem or subject at hand."
> Evans Woollen, architect

Understanding your internal clock and your work rhythms is helpful. My friend Karen works intensely from 11:00 a.m. to 6:00 p.m. "I can show up before 11, but nothing's going to get done." My nephew and my mother work best in the middle of the night.

Knowing your rhythms and having a routine helps, but know that it will vary—either because you need something different or because life intrudes. "Artists often set some kind of schedule for themselves and feel that the regular rhythm of daily involvement is essential," said Anna Held Audette. "The important thing is to work as much as possible."

She doesn't mean you should work non-stop all day every day. Most of us can't sustain creative effort for long periods over endless days. Understand your limits.

> "I am working as much as I can. People who have managed to do something have followed different paths, but they have never deviated from hard work."
> Joan Miro, artist

Cathy Pickens

On the other hand, don't get derailed when you can't put in your optimal hours every day. And don't beat yourself up or penalize yourself. At one point, if I didn't meet my page goal by the end of the day, I'd add those pages to the next day. Big mistake. I found I just fell farther behind and felt worse about my efforts.

Every day is a new day. If you've set realistic goals based on your rhythms and stamina and time constraints, start afresh tomorrow. No looking back.

Even though you may miss some days or your routine is sidelined by life, doing *some* work every day is vital, even if it is only mental attention to what you *want* to do when you have time to work.

Flow

The ultimate benefit of routine is an almost-other-worldly state called *flow*. Researcher Mihaly Csikszentmihalyi has conducted countless studies and authored several books on the subject. Flow is a pleasant state, where you are fully immersed in an activity and lose track of time. The creative equivalent of a "runner's high," it is a state devoutly to be wished for. The work is going so well, it's almost effortless. It is "flowing" from you.

Creativity expert Rollo May described it as being absorbed: "'Absorption, being caught up in, wholly involved,' and so on, are used commonly to describe the state of the artist or scientist when creating or even the child at play. By whatever name one calls it, genuine creativity is characterized by an intensity of awareness, a heightened consciousness."

According to Csikszentmihalyi's research, flow is easiest to enter when you have three elements:

❶ "Clear set of goals that require appropriate responses" like games with rules or a musical composition or surgery—not unorganized, messy enterprises like normal life. These goals can be a certain number of pages, an amount of time at the easel or interviewing experts—anything against which you can measure your effort.

❷ "Immediate feedback" so you know how you're doing. Again, this can be met with measurable daily goals, which will change for each stage of a project.

❸ Your skills are "fully involved in overcoming a challenge that is *just about* manageable"—not too hard so that you become frustrated or anxious, not too easy so you become "relaxed, then bored."

Csikszentmahihalyi said, "To experience flow continuously, one must keep cultivating interest and curiosity, respond to a wide range of opportunities, and develop as many skills as possible." Sound familiar? Isn't this what you've been doing?

Once you've experienced flow, fully immersed where the work is moving on its own, where you become almost an observer, you will want to return to that place time after time. It is a delicious euphoria.

How can you achieve this state?

First, set goals for yourself. A certain amount of time at the computer or drawing board, a certain number of pages drafted or edited, a certain time spent thinking or planning—time or output are usually the easiest goals to measure.

Second, show up at the same time, the same place, every day.

It's that simple.

Some days, you sit staring into space. But the more regularly you show up, with work at hand, the more easily you will find yourself slipping into flow.

I have found this to be true in my own writing. I show up the same time, the same place, every day—or I try to. Some days, I slip easily into the work. On other days, I struggle to squeeze words off the end of my pen, convinced the entire day is a waste. I don't leave until that day's pages are finished, though. The surprise comes weeks or months later, when I begin rewriting. Amazingly, when reading the manuscript, I can't tell the days that felt productive from the days that felt like failures. It was an epiphany to realize that doing the work was what was important—not my emotional state or the weather or if I had a headache or wanted to be somewhere else.

Writer Natalie Goldberg says the secret for writers is "to keep their hands moving and to work for prescribed lengths of time. This exercise works for visual artists, too. While creativity may be an unpredictable unknown, the rules for the exercise concern two very controllable elements: physical activity and a given length of time."

Some take "setting measurable goals" quite seriously. Novelist and teacher Marcie Hershman said, "Sometimes I use the kitchen stove timer. On days when I don't want to write, I go set the timer on the stove to go for sixty minutes. I say to myself, You only have to write till the buzzer goes off, and then I work this hour, and I set it again. My mother used to set a timer for me when I practiced the piano, I think that was the source of this thing. It didn't help me be a good piano player but it helped me have discipline, and that's good for all the arts."

A routine time and place in which you allow yourself to become focused and absorbed in your work may be the key element that defines productive creatives. "When you are completely caught up in something," said creativity expert Rollo May, "you become oblivious to things around you, or to the passage of time. It is this absorption in what you are doing that frees your unconscious and releases your creative imagination." This freedom, though, comes only with the discipline of showing up ready to work.

Nibbling

I've encouraged you to set goals for what you'll do every day—either the amount of time or amount of output. To do this, you must study yourself and your work and experiment until you find what works best. For me, I can usually write three to five pages a day; when editing later drafts, ten or even fifty pages a day may be possible, depending on how far along I am in the process. For planning, I set aside an amount of time (usually two to four hours at a time).

For more complicated or lengthier projects you may need to break your project into more manageable pieces. I think of this as "nibbling," taking it in small, digestible bits.

You may want to be very specific about what you'll work on, what stage you're in, and how long you expect it to take. Or you may need to divide the work into things you need to do when you are fresh (like paint or edit a draft) and things you can do at your less productive times of day (stretch canvases, do research, return phone calls).

Breaking work into smaller pieces and scheduling those pieces may be skills you'll need to practice, but you'll find it much less daunting if you see a project in attackable bits.

For writers, I remind them that on average it takes only fifteen minutes to handwrite a 250-word, 8½-x-11-inch page. If you write only a page a day (fifteen minutes' worth of work), you'll have a book manuscript at the end of the year. That year will pass one way or another; whether you have a manuscript at the end of it or not is up to you. Might as well start nibbling away at it.

Interruptions and Multi-Tasking

In our hyperkinetic culture, many of us pride ourselves on our ability to multitask, to efficiently juggle multiple items at the same time. Brain scientists just snicker at the thought.

Because of the corpus callosum's function as the brain's traffic cop between its two hemispheres, our cognitive functions are relatively linear. We are not really handling multiple tasks; we are, at best, switching quickly between tasks. Women are generally better at switching rapidly from one task to another, which is a good thing since, in evolutionary terms, Mom could gather food, keep an eye on the baby, and look for saber tooth tigers at the same time. Still, we get more done if we concentrate on one task at a time, rather than doing multiple tasks. High-schoolers, for example, take longer finishing their homework if they are listening to music and text-messaging friends at the same time, rather than focusing on their math problems.

Research shows it can take from fifteen minutes to an hour to become fully refocused on a task after an interruption. Our willingness to allow frequent interruptions affects our ability to do deep thinking and analysis so that interruptions lead to shallow, superficial solutions.

Interruptions at the beginning or the end of a task can be the most harmful. Csikszentmihalyi argues that it is more efficient and effective to work on a task until you are fatigued or stuck before switching to another task. Then the switching serves to refresh your thought processes rather than interrupt them.

The benefits of getting a drink of water, taking a walk, sharpening pencils, or turning to another quick task have become the stuff of legendary a-ha moments. In the mythology of creativity, the breakthrough is magical; the answer just appears while you're doing something else. In reality, the a-ha always comes after the struggle with a problem, when the stepping away allows the brain to surface a solution.

> "I bet you thought that producing creative work was singularly dependent on your ability to think creatively. We should be so lucky. Designers who are successful at producing truly innovative work are masters at controlling the creative process."
>
> Mark Oldach, designer

Control over your time and over the projects in which you invest your time and energy are important keys to maximizing your creative activity. As Csikszentmihalyi observed in his research, "In many jobs, constant interruptions build up a state of chronic emergency and distraction. Stress is not so much the product of hard work, as it is of having to switch attention from one task to the other without having any control over the process."

As we discussed in the chapters on capturing and rambling, the time and the freedom to explore your own ideas is imperative—and creativity research bears that out.

"The manager who does not set some time aside for reflection every day is likely to be headed for a burnout," said Csikszentmihalyi. "And the manager who does not actively protect his subordinates' psychic energy from being disrupted is going to have a frustrated staff. It takes trust to respect a closed door, or private space in the maze of cubbyholes; but the manager who encourages workers to set a 'Do Not Disturb' policy when necessary is not likely to regret it."

☛ GROUCHINESS. A word of warning, delivered on behalf of those with whom you are closest. You may not succumb to this particular malady, but just in case, you and those who love you may need to be aware.

Some of us in the throes of a creative project don't like to be interrupted. When we are interrupted, we can be grouchy. Given what you know about *flow* and the deep concentration it represents, this should come as no surprise.

However, I must admit I'm surprised how snippy and short-tempered and pettish I can become when I'm interrupted. I shouldn't act that way. My husband seldom interrupts, and I can usually wall myself off from others quite easily. I don't have a phone in my study, and I don't let my email chirp at me. But whether things are going well or too slowly, whether the interruptions are frequent or only when the house is on fire, breaks in concentration are tough.

Do your best to keep interruptions at bay for a reasonable period of time every day. And continue to be nice to those who love you, even when they break into your concentration to warn you the house is on fire. You will eventually open the door and it would be nice if your loved ones still love you when you reappear.

Hard Work Ahead

When it is time to act, you must continue to wrestle your ideas into a usable shape. You can't know what you have until you sit down and spend time with it. You need to recognize this: *It is hard work for everyone, not just for you.*

> "I assumed that creative people are just creative. One thing I learned during this class is that creativity doesn't just happen. It takes hard work, tremendous effort, risk, failure, determination, and dedication among others. We see famous artists, painters, musicians, photographers, composers, etc. as creative people with natural abilities. We see their successes and think that it just comes so easily and naturally to them. In fact, if we know their story, their creativity is anything but an easy process."
>
> R.B., workshop student

Congressman and songwriter Ed Zschau talked about writing songs as a hobby: "But when I get up from that, I'm exhausted. The creative process is hard. It's hard to be creative. It's hard to work because you have to push yourself into the unknown, to take risks. It's so much easier to do something the way everyone has always done it—and that's why I think that most of the time most people aren't very creative."

As you set to work, don't expect it to be quickly finished. Don't expect the path to be clear. You've only just begun to work. Approach it with the playful, open attitude you experienced while rambling. Give it the dedication and work ethic a child gives to making mud pies or pine needle forts. "Sooner or later, one has to make decisions," said researchers Jeff Mauzy and Richard Harriman, "but new ideas don't come full blown and ready to be accepted or rejected. They need to be explored, modified, and tailored before anyone can make a fair decision about their worth."

> "A lot of people have creative ideas, but when they try and it does not come out like they expected it to, then they feel they are not creative."
> R.K., workshop student

Judgment, evaluation, revision, these all come later. Now you are finding out what you have—and what you need. You don't know how it will turn out, but your vision should exceed your grasp. Not to an impossible or demoralizing degree, but enough to keep you challenged and seeking.

The production of a creative work does not come all at once. Writers smile in recognition at the adage, "I don't like writing. I like having written," because it is work to make the translation from what I'd like to say to what I am able to say. The two—the idealized and the realized—are not always the same. I cannot always achieve what I set for myself to do, so the attempt can be exhausting.

But even getting close can be exhilarating.

I use writing to illustrate the creative process because that's where I work most often. The basics apply, though, wherever you do your creative work.

I find it helpful to pick a date when I will begin each stage of a project, starting with the Engage stage. I find that research and planning can turn into a synonym for "procrastination." So I set a date when I'll begin to "act," when my fanny will find a seat and I'll pick up my pen and start writing. I do the same when it's time to rewrite or tweak. The outline of the process provides a road map; goals and deadlines keep me moving.

None of these stages are set in stone. If I want, I can move back to the cogitate or ramble or Engage stages, even after I've started on a project. Those engaged in the creative process don't say, "Oh, I can't rethink an idea or do more research; I've already moved past that stage." Designating stages, giving them names, and recognizing their distinct elements is merely an attempt to explain a fluid process that is unique to each person and to each project. However, it helps to recognize the framework because, without a disciplined approach, tackling a project can be overwhelming.

I've heard many writers say every creative project is different and presents its own challenges. If I could follow a recipe—five pages today, exactly ten characters stirred in, a tincture of suspense, bake for three months in the first draft phase—then I'd be stamping out cookie-cutter shapes, not writing something new or challenging myself to be better at my craft.

As Gertrude Stein observed, "If you knew it all it would not be creation but dictation. No book is a book until it is done, and you cannot say that you are writing a book while you are just writing on sheets of paper and all that is in you has not yet come out." That's true whether you are creating a book or a credit card campaign or new dining room curtains.

However, recognizing the distinct phases of the process helps remind us that the process has a natural ebb and flow, a broad-stroke outline we can use as a touchstone during those times when we lose sight of our landmarks, where the ideas and the process are not flowing smoothly.

The Slough of Despond

For me, when I hit a certain part of the first draft—around the half to three-quarters mark—I sometimes derail. I can't remember why I thought this idea would work or what I've already said or where I thought I was going. Sometimes I have to do something that feels backward—for instance, I might build an outline of a manuscript I'm already deep into working on—to get myself back on track. From other writers, I know this feeling is common. Novelist Lawrence Block said it usually hit him a little over halfway through a first draft.

Those working in other fields report similar experiences. "Self-doubt may begin to creep in as you proceed," said artist Peggy Hadden. "Something is not right here. What to do? Well, you can start over, or you can see where these different decisions will lead you. If something you had planned changes, follow along to see where it leads…. As you work, mistakes will occur. That is inevitable. Because making art is about choices, some choices will be the wrong ones. We artists make lots of mistakes. It's part of what we do."

Knowing I've hit this same spot before—and knowing that other artists hit the same bump, oddly enough at about the same point in their manuscripts or work—is reassuring. The reassurance alone doesn't get me over the bump, but it does let me know that if I keep pushing I'll move past it.

However, at some points, you may have to quit pushing. You may need to take a step back and reassess. Most of the time, pushing through the tough parts is the key, but if it becomes clear you are getting nowhere, you have options: switch to another task, or approach this one from another direction, or change your work habits for a day or two. Do some more research. Ask more questions.

Don't just go through the motions or, as John Ruskin said, "get the thing done…. The true zeal and patience of a quarter of an hour are better than the sulky and inattentive labour of a whole day." The Act stage of the CREATE! process—like those that come before—involves striking a balance: Push or relax? Rethink or stick with it?

No magic formula can tell you when to push through and when to step away to gain perspective. I will warn you, though, about a tendency to "skitter away" just when the work hits a snag, needs more thinking, or isn't flowing. Be aware of how quickly you want to dance away when it gets tough. Try to hold yourself to the task, but if nothing is coming, turn to something else for a short while, whether a walk, a phone call, or another task. You'll be more refreshed, and you may have incubated a solution. But return to work you must.

"How long should this process go on? As long as your schedule permits.... Minimally, this process might take a few hours. Optimally, it should take a few days. It could even take a few weeks, if you have that much time. When you can let the information stew for more than a few days, review the information every couple of days.... The more you create, the more you understand the way your own mind works. Different people brainstorm and process ideas differently. Know what fires your imagination, and set the stage every time you are ready to create."

Mark Oldach, designer

The "It's All Crap" Stage

There is one stage of the creative process I've avoided talking about, one that comes after you've begun to act, after you've created something you can reflect on. I lovingly refer to this as the "it's all crap" stage of the creative process. This is the time when my husband is most likely to hear me dragging around the house moaning: "It's awful! I'll never finish! It's the worst thing I've ever done! I'll never write again!"

Writers can be very dramatic.

If I thought I was the only writer—the only person—who ever wallowed in the Slough of Despond during a project, I would never dare tell you about it. I would stay mum about my sad little histrionic secret.

However, I'm not typically given to histrionics. I'm typically a sensible, organized, practical person…for a writer. I also know I'm not the only one who regularly experiences the "it's all crap" phenomenon during a project.

This will most likely occur when you begin tweaking or re-working a project, but I mention it here so you'll be forewarned. It can be a rough stage, whenever it strikes. Harper Lee reportedly threw the manuscript for *To Kill A Mockingbird* out the window of her third-floor New York City walk-up into the snow-covered alley. Fortunately for her readers, she walked down and retrieved it and continued to rework it.

By the umpteenth time I go through the manuscript, after I've made it as good as I thought I could, after my first readers have torn it apart and I've licked my wounds and then listened to their advice and gone back through it three, four, five *more* times, then and only then do I begin to see a glimmer that it might be okay. The crap phase can be a long one.

I'm never quite convinced it's good enough, though. Even after my editor and copy editors have gone through it and given it back to me for even more go-throughs, even after reviewers begin to post judgments on it (and even when those are good), even then I'm not satisfied.

Leonardo da Vinci observed, "Art is never finished, only abandoned." Eventually the book will be taken away from me, and I'll move on to another project, convinced I can make the next one closer to the ideal in my head (which is the Expand stage of our creative process).

Deadlines and Other Dreaded Constraints

Most of us like to imagine a creative life of open-ended freedom, unbounded by constraints of time and money. That may be why many artists have such fond memories of art school— supplies and equipment readily at hand, time to work (though never enough time to sleep), and compatriots consumed by the same creative passion. Even at school, though, deadlines provide boundaries and motivation.

Ironically, even when we chafe at their constraints, boundaries can spark creativity. Plays and movies are written within the boundary of three acts. Japanese haiku poetry is limited to only 17 syllables or sound units on three structured lines. Traditional murder mysteries must introduce all the characters early in the book and give all the clues while keeping the reader guessing who-dunnit. The boundaries not only *confine* but also *define* many art forms.

Many creative people see the value of constraints, whether money or time. Diane McKee, the president of the Creative Content Division of Cirque du Soleil, said, "Oh, we've got budgets and deadlines, all right," she said. "Without them, I don't think we'd be half as creative as we are. They force us to come up with solutions we'd never think of otherwise. Constraints on time, money, and resources can be incredible motivators! Some of our most inspired ideas have arisen from the most Spartan situations."

☛ THE PROSPECT OF BEING HANGED. Dancer/choreographer Twyla Tharp found the value of constraints in her creative life. "I've seen too many artists dry up the moment they had enough money in the bank."

She recounts a time when she developed a production with austere resources that had followed quickly on the heels of another where she had a wealth of resources. Looking back on the production with limited resources, she found it was "an ideal situation for me. With a constricted timetable, bare-bones budget, and dancers I couldn't count on to be at my beck and call, I responded accordingly. The circumstances demanded total self-reliance and exquisite planning.... The conditions were so limited that, as Samuel Johnson said about the prospect of being hanged, they concentrate the mind wonderfully."

Constraints come in many shapes and sizes. While money is important, time is the resource most often in short supply for both professional and avocational creatives. One of the best ways to manage too little time is to decide to get started. Plan what you need to do and on what timetable. Set your own deadlines, even when no one is demanding that you do. In other words, ponder and wander about, but don't let your planning go on forever. Decide when and how you will eventually engage in your project. Set a deadline for when you will act. Deadlines become your creative best friend.

Bernard Lavallard, an inaugural member of Cirque du Soleil's coaching staff, said of deadlines: "Of course, they always come too fast, but without them, your mind is not focused. With them, on the other hand, your panicked mind starts coming up with crazy ideas it never would have otherwise."

☞ "One of the core myths about creativity and innovation is that they require freedom from constraint," said researchers Nicholas Ind and Cameron Watt. "There are always constraints.... Freedom needs order to be successful. Our research among highly creative organizations shows that understanding their constraints provides a focus for their creativity."

Learning to give yourself deadlines and to work within other constraints sets you apart from those who simply wish they were productive. The Act stage is where you master the discipline of focus, of pushing through, of striking a balance, of seeing the work as more important than your emotional response to it.

"At the end of the day, good engineers ship," said Twyla Tharp, referring to Tracy Kidder's account of the computer developers in his book *The Soul of A New Machine*. "In other words," she said, "while perfection is a wonderful goal, there comes a point where you have to let your creation out into the world or it isn't worth a tinkerer's damn."

Experiments

At this stage, you should be involved in your own project or problem. Now it's time to *act* on your own.

❑   Experiment with how much work you get done on an average day. That will vary according to where you are in a project, but study your own rhythms.

❑   Set realistic goals (time or output) for your workdays, and be willing to modify those goals as needed. Challenge yourself just enough—but not too much. Most important: get busy with your own work.

Cathy Pickens

Chapter 7

Tweak

Deep down inside, all those engaged in creative work harbor a dream that the work will emerge perfect, that both creator and audience will greet it as a masterpiece, the magnum opus. But experienced travelers along the creative path know even a magnum opus is unlikely to be greeted as such when it first stands in the doorway to meet the world.

We want it to be easy (or at least finished), but even when we would like to be finished, we know we aren't. Not yet. Poet John Ciardi spoke of a mindset among some writers "that the impromptu was what happened when you sat down and let it spill, whereas I find over the years that the impromptu is what begins to happen slowly at the tenth, fifteenth, or twentieth draft." The tweaking stage is when we work through those twenty or so drafts.

To *tweak* an idea or project is to revise it—or to "re-vision" it, to see it anew with fresh eyes, to see it from varying perspectives.

Difficult as it is to realize, even after much tweaking, the work won't be perfect. It may delight its creator and many others, but can reality ever match the initial perfect conception in the mind's eye? That's as it should be. Who, once perfection has been achieved, would continue the difficult work of creating? We create because we want to continually test our skills against the ideal in our mind—the striving is often the real purpose. After all, at the heart of a true creative process, it is the work itself—testing the balance of challenges and skills—that drives us.

Once we accept the difficulty—the impossibility—of perfection, we can relax and go on with "gradually weeding out the parts that aren't good...." You learn what works, eventually.

When we reach this point in the process, we realize the reality does not exactly match our mental ideal. In addition, once we've opened the door and allowed others to see our work, we also find that what made sense to us as we created doesn't necessarily make sense to our reader, viewer, audience, or boss.

It Takes a Village to Create

Unless you are creating purely for your own pleasure, you will eventually want an audience. The culmination of most creative acts is when the result—the painting, book, invention, business idea, and so on—interacts with another human mind. I'm always struck by the strange and magical process by which something takes shape in my brain and is then transmuted using squiggles on a page into a form that can be uploaded by another human brain and reconstituted into a semblance of the story I saw in my head.

Not exactly the same story, though. The reader brings her own experience, her perceptions, her shades of meaning. Without the reader, do I really have a story? Doesn't it take *both* of us to create the experience?

Unless I write my story and hand it directly to a single reader, the process will involve more than two people. Few creative activities are performed in isolation. The broader the audience, the more varied the interpretations. The more commercial the output, the more brains stirring the pot (to mix the metaphors).

Before one of my mysteries hits bookstore shelves, a group of carefully chosen first readers see it, as do a technical expert or two, my agent, my editor, a copy editor, a typesetter, and many other people whose names and jobs I don't even know. All of them played a part in making sure the story I tried to capture traveled to readers in as coherent and entertaining a package as we could craft. The story was mine, but could readers' brains translate it in a way that made sense? All those folks helped make sure my story didn't falter badly or wander too far afield.

Imagine the number of brains that collaborate on creating a movie, a play, a ride at Disney World, a new banking process, or a community fundraiser. No one involved in such projects can have the solo pride of ownership of, say, a poet who scribbles secretly and hides his foolscap in a desk drawer away from others' eyes— away from collaborators who will bring something of their own that changes the poem. Because as soon as it is out of the drawer and in someone else's hands, it *will* change, if only in the confines of that other brain.

> "Architecture is a much more social act than writing—you have to win over the client. There are extremely talented people who withered in the profession because they weren't outgoing enough to win clients. The actual creation in architecture— the creative time—is, proportionately, seemingly miniscule."
>
> Evans Woollen, architect

Accepting and Rejecting

If you want your creativity to play on the broadest possible stage, to have the deepest impact, you must master two important skills: (1) the ability to accept critique or feedback or input (from yourself as well as from others) and (2) the judgment to know what feedback to use and what to reject.

You must also fight two urges, and these urges are strong. The first is to reject any criticism, idea, input, or feedback directed at a work. All of us would love to have our work unequivocally, widely, wildly, and immediately acclaimed. Doesn't happen. Get over it. Recognizing the value of wise critique is the hallmark of mature, effective creativity.

This urge to reject is often manifested in the "yeah, but..." response. Rather than waiting to hear and digest the feedback, the creator leaps in with an explanation. "Yeah, but that's not..." or "Yeah, but what I meant was...." With creative output, the result has to speak for itself. I cannot follow every reader around and explain, "Now here, this is what I really meant" or "This is what's happening." The words have to be arranged on the page so the story speaks, with no further assistance from me.

The second dangerous urge is less common, in my experience, but just as damaging to good creative work: the urge to take all critique as valid. The result then is either the creator blows in the wind of opinion, trying to address every concern and losing sight of the vision that prompted the project in the first place, or he shuts down and simply abandons his idea.

This urge is usually born of insecurity or lack of faith in one's creative ability. Understanding the process and, with it, your own strengths and abilities can help temper this fear and uncertainty. True, I've seen more writers and other artists succumb to the "I'm right, shut up" error than to the "I'm wrong, I'll go away" error. Maybe, though, that's because the people who simply go away take with them their creative output and no one ever benefits from what it could have become. How sad.

> "A great deal of talent is lost to the world for want of a little courage. Every day sends to their graves obscure men whose timidity prevented them from making a first effort."
>
> Sydney Smith, 19th century clergyman

In short, both responses—either "I'm always right" or "You're always right"—are death knells for effective creativity. In the first instance, others will stop offering advice; they know the creator doesn't play well with others, so they stop accepting his invitations to join him on the playground. In the second instance, he un-invites himself; he takes his marbles—or his short story or his new business process—and slinks back to his garret or cubicle. In both cases, good ideas die.

An important part of the creative process is learning how to accept, weigh, incorporate, and discard feedback. We must learn how to listen to others—and when to listen to ourselves.

How do you master this? Experience.

How to Tweak Your Own Work

The first "tweaks" or evaluation and revising of our work should be done in private. Stephen King encourages writers to keep the study door closed and do their initial drafts in private. This is good advice for most creative endeavors. When it is as good as you think you can make it, then you may open the door, but carefully.

Once you have engaged with your ideas or your material and you've done the work, you need to step away from it and study it. When you think you've finished, you will be tempted to walk to the door and fling it wide open, to see what others think of your work. Resist that urge. You aren't ready yet. Be patient.

> "If what you are making is open to scrutiny all the time, you won't permit yourself to work through difficult periods."
>
> Anna Held Audette, artist

One surprise to those new to the creative path is that most of us are seldom happy or satisfied with what we have created—especially in these initial stages of the revision process.

> "I too often tell myself: 'It's not quite there yet. You can do better.' I can rarely keep myself from redoing a thing—umpteen times the same thing. Sometimes it gets to be a real obsession. After all, why work otherwise, if not to better express the same thing? You must always seek perfection."
>
> Pablo Picasso, painter

Another surprise? How long professionals delay before they share their work with others. At first, we are excited and want to share our new idea or creation. Experience, though, teaches us to temper our enthusiasm and—yes, embarrassingly true—our need for affirmation.

When you think your work is finished, proceed carefully. Especially in the initial stages, ideas are fragile, vulnerable to criticism, easily sidetracked or co-opted or killed. In a burst of enthusiasm, in the first blush of energy around something new, we want to share it. But this is not a restaurant you discovered or a movie you enjoyed. This is a newborn creation. Keep it inside until it is ready to safely venture out into a harsh world.

Even if no one punctures your idea balloon when you first float it, you may find that, after you've talked about it, your enthusiasm evaporates. Once you've spent your creative energy discussing it, you may have no more interest in developing that idea into a completed work.

When I was first told that writers shouldn't discuss their ideas, I thought that an odd warning. Since then, I've seen the wisdom of that advice because I've known those who don't produce much. They have plenty of ideas, but they spend themselves in talking, not in the hard work of translating their ideas to a more permanent, polished form.

This isn't to say that you won't or can't do creative work in groups. Many creative projects are developed in collaborative settings. However, while you are developing your *individual* creative process, you need to experiment with protecting your initial ideas and actions. You will find the balance between private work and collaboration that's best for you, but for now, you are learning how *you* work.

Once you've completed a project, when it is time to gather feedback, another problem may arise. I've known those who produce but never share. Perhaps they've been battered and damaged in the past, but whatever the reason, they write or play music or paint only for themselves. That's not a waste, but it could well be a loss. Who knows what they have to offer?

We all must find the balance between rushing out too quickly and hiding behind our studio or office door. The key is to understand the different stages of the creative process.

After the Act stage, when you have created a work, the first step in revision is doing nothing. Give yourself some down-time. Put the work aside. Leave it alone. For how long? For as long as it takes. Stephen King likes to go fishing for a couple of days after finishing a novel and then work on something else for a minimum of six weeks before he returns to the draft. A short item may need to lie fallow for only a day. For a major project, maybe a month. Some projects may require years.

☛ In my business life, I developed projects that weren't adopted. For some of these ideas, the timing, interest, and funds came together later; some may stay filed away forever. Not all ideas are good ones. Or maybe they aren't right for that time or place.

My first novel isn't the one that was published; that first one resides in the bottom drawer of my filing cabinet along with drafts of two kids books that also didn't work. When I say no work is ever wasted, I know from experience. I started those projects with every intention they would be published and every hope they would be successful. I learned a lot from working on them, but I'm very grateful they didn't make it into the world. Who wants to live down flawed work?

During this downtime away from your project, you may work on something completely different. As an example, I revise a writing project only after I have set it aside (about a month for a book), organized closets, cleaned out my email inbox, or worked on something that uses a different part of my brain. A painter friend writes poetry; another makes jewelry before she returns to evaluate a painting.

Recognize that ideas or projects need to incubate. You must give yourself distance, so you can see it with new eyes. When you are first rambling around a project, it is helpful and freeing to remember you can always change it later. At this tweaking stage, you must be *willing* to change it. Don't settle on one solution too quickly.

When I first I return to the draft of a book, I move through it quickly. I want to get an overview first, look for holes that need to be filled, inconsistencies. In each pass through the work, I isolate different elements and focus on those. I want to see the big picture, to see if the structure is in place, which is very important for a puzzle mystery with its traditional play-fair-with-the-reader format.

The next readings are a slow, slogging process, several months of combing through the work in finer and finer detail. This takes longer than writing the initial draft. I tear everything apart, every word, every scene. I keep running lists of items I need to research, points that need to be connected to plot points earlier or later in the story. (Remember that, for me, this is *after* a lot of time spent planning and outlining in the Engage phase.)

Additional read-throughs will isolate different elements, including consistency, logic, and pacing. I set a number of pages to complete each day, to keep myself moving. At a late point in the process, I'll read it aloud to see what I've missed.

I may go through a piece fifteen or twenty times, focusing on different aspects, before I even think about sharing it with anyone else. (It's such fun to read the same book twenty times, especially when you know how it ends!)

How does a writer's work compare with other kinds of creative work? At its essence, the process doesn't differ in any significant way. Photographers, for example, take lots of photographs, study others' photographs, train themselves to identify what they like in a photo and why it works. From studying others' work, they train their own internal editors, which they then focus on their own work. They take lots of shots no one else ever sees. Scientists experiment and make notes, evaluate, and try again.

Painters do practice sketches or studies, repeatedly exploring the same subject.

☞ PERSONAL BEST. In the Ramble and Engage stages, you've played with and studied the work of others in your field. Be careful, though, about measuring your work against that of others. The goal in studying their work is to train your internal editor, to educate your judgment, to decide for yourself what works, what doesn't, and why. You need to educate yourself about your chosen field. You need benchmarks—which you may accept and build on or reject in favor of a new vision. But you should measure your current work and its growth against your previous work, not against someone else's. Are you improving? Are you stretching yourself?

You have filled your toolbox with tools you've learned from others, both as an observer and a student. You have worked as hard as you know how and taken the work as far as you can. You've polished and refined until you think you can do no more. When the time comes for you to open the door and share your work, understand that you must be ready to accept criticism.

It's not always easy to hear criticism or to know what to do with it—but it does get easier with experience.

To keep your perspective, remember critique is a part of the process—only a part. Once, one of my "first readers" returned one of my manuscripts with apologies that she'd torn my book apart. Before I could fret about what a mess it must be, it struck me: Would I rather hear it from her, when I trust her judgment, when I know she cares about my work, and—most importantly—when I still have a chance to fix it? Or would I rather hear about it from my editor after I've shipped it off with a sigh of relief, thinking it was finished? Or—horrors—would I rather have the flaws held bare by a snarky book reviewer?

Trust me, the more you master the art of tweaking your own work and opening yourself up to the trusted critique of others, the easier it gets to receive critique. Having the flaws pointed out is never as much fun as hearing glowing praise, but it's a valuable part of the process.

The more knowledgeable feedback you receive, the better you will be at anticipating those reactions in your future work. You may find other potholes to fall into as you expand your reach, but your work will improve. For me, I often hear the voices of my long-time first readers echoing in my head as I work. It gets a little crowded in my head at times, but those voices have forced me to improve.

Once you've done all you can, go ahead, open the door. But open it carefully at first…just a crack.

Accept Tweaking From Others

After you've taken the project as far as you can on your own, it's time to see how others see it. As a first step, I suggest you "invite in" a carefully selected group to review your work. Using this select group—call them "validators" (Twyla Tharp), "first readers" (Stephen King), critique or feedback partners, the brain trust, whatever you like—is a step in the creative lives of professional artists that amateurs ignore at their peril.

How do creative professionals use their feedback groups?

Filmmakers use screening audiences before a film is released to test reactions, sometimes presenting the audience with multiple endings or scene options. Playwrights workshop a script to see how it sounds and how others respond. Engineers often work in collaborative groups that discuss and refine a new design; Edison's lab involved almost constant interaction and testing of his ideas with others.

Dancer and choreographer Twyla Tharp invites a small group in to see her work in progress: "My criteria for these validators is very basic: I pick people who (a) have talents I admire greatly (so I know they have judgment), (b) happen to be my friends (so I know they have my best interests at heart), (c) don't feel they are competing with me (so I know they have no agenda no matter what they say), and (d) have hammered my work in the past (so I know they are capable of brutal honesty)."

Stephen King's first reader—and primary audience—is his wife, the novelist Tabitha King, but he also sends his manuscripts to between four and eight other readers to get their subjective feedback. He chooses his readers and values their impressions, but he recognizes that he is still the author; what happens in his book is his call.

Others use a working group while they are developing material. A working group needs to have a clear purpose (or purposes) in mind: To hold members accountable to a work schedule? To review works in progress? To review (almost) finished products with an informed eye? To commiserate? To inform members about opportunities, give business advice, give support during rejection or periods of stagnation or waiting? To socialize? If members want all the above, the group may need to separate its functions. Have dinner before the meeting or meet for a separate luncheon to socialize; good critique requires focus.

I've worked with a group of women in a writing critique group for over twenty years. We have varied backgrounds, but we "grew up" together in our writing, bringing different skills and experiences to our reading of each other's work.

Sometimes the only response we could offer was, "This isn't working. I don't know why, but I stumbled here. I can't see it. I don't believe it. But I don't know how to fix it, either." Even without suggestions for a solution, the recognition of a problem was valuable feedback.

For our group, early on we established the "No 'Yeah, But...' Rule." No one could respond to criticism with, "yeah, but what I was trying to say was..." or "yeah, but you don't understand...." If the writer's intentions weren't clear or weren't working on the page, no amount of explanation to the group was going to make it better. We can ask questions for clarification, but we can't defend. Instead, it's more productive to listen—and process later.

We sometimes go home and lick our wounds. I copy all their written comments onto a master copy, so I can see their reactions as a whole. Most of the time, I have to admit to a problem when three people zero in on the same issue. I can also see the problem more clearly—even if the solution takes time to wrestle through—once I have the benefit of eyes that are not as blind to the faults as mine are. I don't always accept their solutions, though hearing proposed solutions often sparks yet another way to answer the objection or fix the hole.

A good group of evaluators or a good mentor will help you eventually develop to the point where your best critic is in your head. Ideally you will grow to need external critique less, but I can't imagine that artists reach a point where they never need informed developmental feedback.

As a collateral benefit from our group, I learned much about how to write from critically reading my partners' work. Why did I stumble here when reading? What did not ring true? Why was I bored or lost? Wrestling with that in someone else's work, paying attention as they try to upload their story into my brain, makes it easier to recognize similar bumps and detours in my own work.

I also learned to put myself in the seat of the person receiving criticism—how nice it was to hear the good things, but how important it was to hear the bad. Those tough, mean women have saved me from looking idiotic more times than I can count.

The discipline of meeting regularly also made us very productive. At a time when we had no publishing contract deadlines looming to drive us to our desks, we had each other prodding us to produce and to polish.

Our writers' group also became a support and a celebration. We were there with a book-shaped cake for the first big book offer—and also there when it was withdrawn (because the publisher needed the money to buy a big-name book that later flopped, a bittersweet irony). Members have come and gone. For several years, we stopped meeting every month, but even then, we didn't send something out without the group's critique and advice. For an individual project, we may review the whole manuscript, rather than reading it chapter by chapter, setting aside a long day to discuss the book at a single sitting. We also gather because we inspire and spur each other. Our process has morphed as our work has changed, but we're enjoying "growing old" together in our craft.

Forming a Critique Group

I was already published before I found my critique partners, so don't put your creative work on hold while you search for the perfect group. Because I have had a good experience, I recommend building a dedicated, long-term critique group. Others, though, change their critique partners, depending on the project. Some have a single person who serves as a sounding board. Still others, following a horrible experience, have sworn off any permutation of a feedback group. In other words, a group or a partner isn't a requirement, but it can be a valuable part of the process. Do what works for you.

Clarify why you want or need feedback. If you are seeking praise for your magnificent work and overall brilliance, you need to gather a few other like-minded souls who want a pat-on-the-back club and go have some nice refreshments. A group such as that is a waste of everyone's time, though, if you are interested in a serious creative process. No work is perfect. Each of us must develop an open, accepting attitude in both giving and receiving criticism.

On the other hand, some groups—and some creative careers—are derailed by members who take delight in belittling others or pontificating unproductively. Because you should avoid toxic people in your feedback group (and your life), I am not a fan of online critique groups *unless* they meet the test of a good face-to-face group. Many find the support and network they need online, but the anonymity of the internet can invite harsh, bloodsucking, cruel commentators who can hit and run with impunity. My warning is not to avoid online critique groups, only to be careful, to be aware of the downsides of the impersonal nature of the medium, and to pick the partners who can help you grow.

To protect against the downside, whether the group is online or in person, thoughtfully choose those who will first see your work. When opening the door and issuing invitations, *be careful*. Later, when you fling the door wide and send your efforts out into the world, you'll receive all manner of comment. Your work is a fair target then. But not now, while it is still a work in progress.

When the door-flinging time comes, you should be ready for what happens. As Brenda Ueland observed, "It is the brutal egotists that survive." (To be fair, though, she also points out that some of us are too sensitive and treasure our own effort exceeding its value: "I must remind you of this: that we writers are the most lily-livered of all craftsmen. We expect more, for the most peewee efforts, than any other people." So, as always, we must seek a balance.)

You are in the process of developing your thick skin, of becoming a "brutal egotist." Good critique partners not only make your work better, they also prepare you to accept criticism from a broader, more impersonal audience. Now, though, make certain you are ready for critique. I've seen many novice writers who are anxious to know how they are doing, but neither they nor their projects are really ready for a serious critique. They are looking for reassurance, not input.

If you are dying to know how you are doing, look for a class or a mentor or someone else who is working in your field to talk to. Invite a mentor to lunch to discuss where you are. Remember, though, to be respectful of any creative expert's time—she has her own work to do. Again, at this early stage, don't open the door to critique of your work. Getting a face full of reality when you wanted reassurance may derail your project at an important juncture.

Another reason to make sure you really want feedback: Are you willing to listen and make changes? Again, if you want nothing more than a pat on the back, search out a kind friend. But don't waste others' time if you aren't serious about improving your craft.

☛ ARE YOU SERIOUS? As a favor, I once reviewed the early chapters of a new writer's first book; I also put her in touch with an experienced writer friend of mine who spent hours critiquing those first chapters and advising how to improve the glaring novice mistakes in the manuscript—the kinds of mistakes we all make when we start out. Within only a few weeks, the new writer announced her book has been published. Ta-da! She had paid to publish it—without a word or plot hole changed.

Not that I ever recommend accepting wholesale anyone's suggestions for your work...but not a word altered? With that experience, I realized not everyone is interested in learning his craft and I became very protective of my time and that of my talented, generous friends. Be clear about what you want, what you are ready to hear, and what you are going to use. And please respect the time of those whose advice you seek.

When you are ready for critique partners, how do you find the right ones? Luck plays a part, certainly, but look around in your ramblings—in a class, at a museum, in your office, from a mentor.

Groups often form among students in a class, particularly those who take special-interest non-credit courses; this may be the most common genesis for critique groups. Some groups form around a particular project. As with Twyla Tharp and Stephen King, some are handpicked by the artist for a particular project.

Consider joining an existing organization or class that offers support and feedback in your area of creative interest. Ask around to find these. Look for people with whom you would enjoy working; one or two other people can make a group. Perhaps you could offer to coordinate a critique or brainstorming effort for an organization or work group to which you already belong.

Do you want a long-term working group that meets regularly? Or do you need specialized feedback on a particular project? Do you have something to offer in return? Don't be selfish in commanding others' time without giving something in return. And if you want to be selfish about it, pay for it. Book doctors and coaches, teachers and consultants abound.

Who would you like to have in your group? How many members? Two or three members may be enough; fifteen will be too many. You want to have diverse points of view but not too many to manage. Decide also at what stage in their individual creative processes the members should be: Just beginning? Accomplished but ready for something new? I have a bias for members who work in the same field or genre and for including members who are at the same level of development. Of course, it is also possible to have a successful group with a variety of interests and at a variety of levels; a one-room schoolhouse or smorgasbord approach has its advantages, too.

You will be tempted to seek membership in a group that has progressed beyond your own level so you can "network," but that might not be the best place to develop your skills. And what would you bring to the table to benefit those more experienced members?

> One workshop student found the critique process in his photography class helpful, so he asked an experienced photographer friend if he could join his professional critique group. "They were way ahead of me, doing things I wasn't up to yet. I got a clear sense of the divide between us. And I doubt they were glad to have me there. I found some others from my class and we formed a group that's much more helpful for us since we're all working through the same things."
>
> R.S., workshop student

Before joining or forming a group, ask yourself, "Do I like these people?" My writers group was the first work group of women friends I'd ever had. My work life had been filled with men, and growing up with three sisters seemed to take care of the need for sisterly companionship. But these bright, funny women, each with a different background and life journey, brought perspectives that have made my writing—and my life—better.

Consider establishing rules for the group. When I was invited to join my writing group, I was told my invitation might be vetoed after the first meeting. They had a firm rule that no one was admitted without everyone's consent. Everyone was actively working on the same genre of books. Everyone committed to read the pages submitted for the next month. Everyone came to the meetings, even if they hadn't submitted anything that month. (Attendance was never a problem, but maybe that was thanks to the bottomless bag of M&Ms.) The critique was developmental—focused on the work, not the writer.

If the group will be reviewing written material, members should submit it to each other far enough ahead of the meeting that others can read and prepare their written comments. Use the discussion time (which is, after all, limited) to explore options or for those topics on which people disagree or for which the creator needs clarification. Line edits or short questions can be written on the manuscript or proposal so the author can mull on them in the quiet of her study. For some suggestions, she may need distance from it before she can really absorb it and use it.

Work should ideally be critiqued in the form it will be received. Paintings, photographs, sculpture are displayed; plays, music, and dance are performed. Writing is delivered as printed words. Some writing groups read work aloud. While reading aloud to yourself or someone else is a helpful part of tweaking a piece, I want to read someone else's work *alone,* with a pencil in my hand and enough time to think about it. I admit a bias here, but reading aloud becomes a performance—and that is not typically how readers encounter a book.

Not everyone will stay in the group. Commitment levels and group dynamics vary. Stay focused on the *purpose* of the group. Time is valuable. Productively creative people resent wasting time.

The group doesn't necessarily have to meet face to face, and every member doesn't have to comment on the project at every stage. Providing critique staggered at different stages might be helpful for a longer, more complicated project.

How to Give Feedback

Critique or feedback is a two-way exchange. To fully develop your creative capacity, you need to master the art of both giving *and* receiving critical feedback. The dividends are worth the investment of time and ego.

:: Pay attention ::

The first step in giving feedback is (perhaps counterintuitively) to *listen*. Pay attention to the creator. Try to genuinely understand the idea or work being presented to you. Don't leap to your solutions or modifications. Digest it first, before you jump in to improve it.

:: Start with the positive ::

How do you give a *meaningful* critique? Some advocate giving a certain number of supportive comments before giving a negative one—maybe four to one. I don't know what the ideal ratio is, but as a group is first learning to use the critique process, the good comments should outweigh the bad.

In our writers group, it was always nice to read where someone had scribbled "good" in the margin. As we grew to trust each other, we spent less of our discussion time on praise. We said little about the good things: we took them for granted. We continued to scribble "good" in the margins where something stood out, but we knew time was limited and we had worked together long enough that we could move quickly to the real purpose of the critique: what needed to be fixed. We did, though, open every critique with comments about what had sparkled in the work. No matter how experienced you are, that's always nice to hear.

:: Be specific ::

Make your statements concrete, not abstract. Simply saying, "This is good" or "I like this" isn't as helpful as "I like how you seed this conflict" or "This opens up a potential market I never thought about" or "This is so vivid, I could smell it."

Given alone, "I don't like it" isn't a helpful response. *Why* don't you like it? *Where* did you get lost? Sometimes, saying: *That* stumped me, *This* caused me to stumble, *Here* it wasn't clear, and the like, is the best we can offer, even if it comes along with "I don't know how to fix it."

:: Ask for guidance ::

Another helpful technique is to ask the creator guiding or "leading" questions if she doesn't offer these on her own. Ask what has presented the most problems or where she doubts her judgment. These should focus the comments on what she needs help with.

:: Suggest, don't rework ::

Understand that others' vision and yours will vary. If you have a suggestion for how to work through a problem or fix something that's not working, offer it, but don't rewrite or re-do others' work or try to direct their efforts unless they ask for suggestions. Consider how you'd like someone to treat your work.

☛ IF YOU'RE ASKED FOR FEEDBACK. Some of us think we're ready for meaningful critique when we aren't. Be aware of this when someone asks you for feedback. One day, an executive I worked with asked me to read an opinion letter he'd written for publication. He asked me, as a writer, for my feedback. I gave him the kind of critique I seek from and give to my writer colleagues. Big mistake. Questions and comments and suggestions scribbled all over it were not at all what he wanted. He simply wanted his work affirmed.

Now, when colleagues ask me to comment on their work, I try to uncover what they want in order to set expectations. I warn them I move my own words around incessantly because, to my mind, nothing is ever perfect. Some people ask my opinion more than once; that particular fellow never again asked me to read anything.

How to Receive Feedback

The first step when receiving feedback? You've heard this before: *listen*. Don't leap to defend your work.

Accept the suggestions as intended—as fresh eyes on your work. Remember, their perspective will mirror a broader audience's response to your work, though they will probably be more frank and more supportive and more knowledgeable than the world at large.

☞ A SYMPTOM. Advice from a New York editor: "If a writer thinks a suggestion is off base, I ask him or her to consider it simply as a *symptom* that something is not working here. The writer's diagnosis of what is wrong and what needs to be done about it may be entirely different from mine—but I hope he will acknowledge that the passage needs attention. (I often used this reframe myself when my deathless catalogue copy or tip sheets came back 'mangled' by the marketing department.

Once I cooled down, I could usually see that my point had been unclear or off-base. Then I could rewrite to my satisfaction and to theirs."

As the creator, you must judge the validity of the feedback. If more than one person doesn't like something or has questions, *listen closely* to that. Difficult people and difficult messages can be valuable. You must learn to check your ego, which is hard because creative work is very personal.

In any critique setting, I remind myself how hard it is to get a manuscript back with scribbles on it—whether it's from my critique group, my editor, a copy editor, an academic journal reviewer, or anybody. Never once have I gotten the single comment we all secretly hope our work will garner: GENIUS. No, instead, I get anywhere from a few to a blackened storm of inked comments, all designed to make my work better. And, almost without exception, they do.

When first learning how to receive critique, it's important to put feedback in its proper place. Study what it all means, to decide whether it has merit. Most of the time—sometimes with modification or compromise—it improves the idea or the work.

Consider the source. Is the commentator knowledgeable? Does she have your best interests at heart? Might he be having a bad day? Do you just have different styles? Are you taking it out of context or being hypersensitive?

Listen to the good as well as the bad. Too often, we dwell on a single bad comment or developmental suggestion and ignore the ten items of specific and glowing praise.

With any criticism, at whatever stage in the process, handle it the way you handle your "first readers"—learn what to listen to and what to ignore. Test your perception and vision, perhaps refine it—but don't blow in the wind. If you do, you aren't clear enough about your own vision. You may need to spend more time with your work, talk to yourself, explore. At the end, you must trust yourself and your judgment.

When critiquing or re-visioning, a place comes where we've gone too far, changed too much, lost sight of the freshness and spontaneity we started with. That is the place where we may need to take a breather and go back to earlier phases in the creative process such as rambling or engaging, to rediscover our direction.

In some cases, a problem can't be easily solved. "Concede that, for the moment, the problem has gotten the best of you," said artist Anna Held Audette. "Renoir is reputed to have said that after one had put a canvas out of sight for three months and had forgotten the trials, one could see it in a fresh light.... [C]onsider putting your problem away for at least two or three weeks, and work on something else in the meantime."

You can learn much from the joint act of giving and receiving critique from a select group with whom you work over a period of time. The act of being critiqued by the same people you have critiqued will change how you approach, comment on, and mentor the work of others. If you sit on high and pass judgments on others below you, knowing they cannot return the favor of critiquing your work, you won't benefit from the full experience. Being critiqued or evaluated by those above you, for whom you can't provide feedback on their efforts, also doesn't teach you how to guide and develop others (as proven by the weak "performance evaluation" systems in many businesses).

Another benefit of learning the fine art of critique: You learn to deal with rejection. For writers, we live by words and also die by words, in the form of rejection letters or bad reviews. Our dreams are words, and their death comes as words—sometimes as generic, soulless, impersonal rejection letters.

Artists, scientists, entrepreneurs all have their own version of rejection letters or reviews. Ironically, I discovered as a writer that the real purpose of rejection letters was to prepare me for success. When books are published, if the author is lucky, the books are *reviewed*. Are you ready for that? I can quote only a few of the good ones, but I really remember the bad one, the one that started, "How do I hate this book? Let me count the ways..." (Okay, upon checking back, that's not the way it started, but that's the way I remember it.)

If you are serious about pursuing a creative life in any venue, you soon recognize that criticism isn't the worst thing that can happen. The worst thing is being ignored, making not a ripple in the smooth pond of public consciousness. A bad review or negative comment means someone took time to pay attention to what you created. Gathering about you those who will help you polish your work will prepare you and your work for a broader audience and all that will bring, both good and bad.

The Evolution of Critique

For those who have trained in the arts, critique is part of their lives, which leads to an interesting aspect of the nature of artists: they tend to be a critical bunch. When critique becomes a part of your normal process, it can be hard to bite your tongue, even when no one has asked your opinion. In part, these trained artists are hard on others because they are hard on themselves. They demand much and constantly more.

Those experienced in the give-and-take of artists' critique develop short cuts and, as a result, can seem harsh and judgmental to the uninitiated. They have been through the process of tearing their work down, testing it, and rebuilding it so many times they can take a shortcut past the overly sensitive parts of themselves and focus on improving the work—and they expect others to do the same.

There's another phenomenon at work here: experienced artists welcome (and offer) constructive, supportive critique because they never feel they're finished learning and developing. They have a vision of perfection they know is unobtainable, one they know they'll spend their lives pursuing and never reach—yet as they approach it, as their skills and vision improve, they move their goal farther away, so their dream always exceeds their grasp. That's not self-defeating; that's the ideal for the experienced artist.

> The need to be aware of where others are in their experience with critique isn't limited to writers and the arts. "I learned if you have something critical to say about a piece of scientific work, it is better to say it firmly but nicely and to preface it with praise of any good aspects of it. I only wish I had stuck to this useful rule. Unfortunately I have sometimes been carried away by my impatience and expressed myself too briskly and in too devastating a manner."
> Francis Crick, Nobel laureate for discovering the double-helical structure of DNA

Some new to critique sometimes misinterpret the experienced artist's quick cut to frankness. They might see it as ego-driven or as mean-spiritedness. In my experience, this is most likely to happen when an artist-type critique is used by the uninitiated (in business, for example, or by those new to the process). Again, an open give-and-take critique means everyone's ideas are on the table. The process doesn't work as well when someone sits in judgment but is never himself judged. One learns how to give when one has received.

If you are building a critique group of any kind, be aware of this evolution, in yourself and within the group. In the early stages, we need to hear more about what's good in our work. We cannot always see what's good as we explore a new technique or develop a new outlet. What is working well needs to be reinforced. Eventually, we need less reinforcement and see more readily the need for improvement.

If new members join your group, people who have not had a chance to develop their ability to give and receive critique, keep in mind they may not be ready for a shortcut jump to what needs fixing. They will need to be reminded the work has good parts before the questions and criticisms fly. They will also need time to learn how to give critique. Remembering to start with the good points helps set a productive tone for a critique meeting. Keep this in mind if you manage people in any setting and explain the process to newcomers.

☞ WHAT IS YOUR DEFAULT SETTING? Tempering my default setting, which is to move immediately to what needs to be fixed, has been a battle within myself. I grew up in a family that tested perceptions constantly. To my husband, it first sounded as though we were arguing with each other (especially my mother and me). After some observation, he saw no anger but plenty of critique. Any statement was followed with, "Well, actually..." and a restatement, addition, or improvement. What sounds to us like a conversation sounds judgmental and critical to someone else. In my family, we accept and recognize each others' talents. We don't need that reinforcement. In dealing with others, though, I have to remind myself that my default setting points out flaws, errors, and weak spots too quickly.

This default setting develops in most people as they gain expertise in any field. After all, accomplished people have seen the rookie mistakes before—heck, we've *made* the rookie mistakes. The faster we point them out, the quicker they're resolved and we can move on to more interesting and challenging problems. We too easily forget our own rookie days. We forget that someone let us make mistakes and learn, if we were lucky. The best mentors—those who encourage creative thinking and guide it to maturity—strike the balance between what is best learned by trial and error and when a shortcut is possible.

The more those with whom you work (and live) discover their own creative process, the more shortcuts you can take. Like learning your way around a new city or mastering a new software package or a new job, with familiarity comes ease. But that takes experience and time. Don't rush into the critique process. Take time to build your own expertise and that of the others in your group—or you'll do more harm than good.

Taking A Risk

The tweaking stage is the time when the thing we most feared becomes reality: *FAILURE*. Somewhere in this stage, we may find what we've labored over simply doesn't work or isn't finished or no one likes it or...

Perhaps fear of failure with a creative act is more intimidating because creative acts expose us in personal ways. But the benefits of failure can be hard for us to see. We fret over and run from the risk of failure. The last thing we would consider is that failure can be a creative friend.

One benefit to failing is finding out we can take a risk that doesn't work and still survive. "Believe me," said dancer Twyla Tharp, "success is preferable to failure. But there is a therapeutic power to failure. It cleanses. It helps you put aside who you aren't and reminds you who you are. Failure humbles."

> "Yes, risk-taking is inherently failure-prone. Otherwise it would be called sure-thing-taking."
> Jim McMahon, former pro football quarterback

Surviving a failure can paradoxically improve our risk-taking skills. Creativity requires risk-taking—going where no one has gone before. When we find out failing isn't nearly as bad as we had feared, the next risk is easier to take.

Failure also teaches us how to deal with setbacks. If we can learn from our mistakes, we may not make fewer mistakes but perhaps we will make more ambitious mistakes. More importantly, we can learn much from discovering how to fix our mistakes.

Cooking impresario Julia Child admitted, "Of course, I made many boo-boos. At first this broke my heart, but then I came to understand that learning how to fix one's mistakes, or live with them, was an important part of becoming a cook."

As we learn to fix our mistakes, we also discover that we need not look for a single perfect solution on the first attempt—or perhaps on any attempt. Few problems have a single solution or one right answer.

Being able to survive, recover from, and use failure is one of the best indicators of success, according to research by the Center for Creative Leadership. How they use failure is a hallmark of successful leaders—and of successful creators. No one likes to fail, but everyone does—at least everyone who tries something risky. *How* we fail is what separates those who eventually succeed from those who don't.

Setbacks in artists' lives are part of the process, whether it's a writer collecting rejection slips, a painter losing out on a gallery slot, or a researcher denied funding. Rejections mean we are at least in the hunt; we're putting ourselves and our work out there, not sitting back wondering "What if...?"

When dealing with failure, ask yourself if you are learning anything. Maybe what you learn is that you're wed to your idea even when it doesn't seem to be a good idea. Your passion can be enlightened true love, or it can be misguided stubbornness. How do you know which?

Discernment is required. How do we get that? By studying our craft, by seeking—and listening to—wise mentors. By continuing to work. Yes, keep polishing that first attempt, but don't make that your only attempt. Have your goal firmly in mind, but test your perceptions against the information you gather from others.

We hear of those who believed in their own genius even when others didn't, whose fame eventually came, sometimes after their lifetimes. But we seldom hear of those who misguidedly clung to the notion of their own genius when, in fact, it wasn't genius at all. The world never did come around. They stopped growing, stopped learning. They didn't move on to other projects.

Robert Kearns, who invented the intermittent windshield wiper (one of my personal favorite car inventions), spent his life trying to get Ford, GM, and Chrysler to pay him for his design and, more important to him, to acknowledge his genius. He spent all his energy and much of his life in a battle with Goliaths, rather than moving on to new ideas. As his son observed after his father's death, what did the world lose because he didn't move on to other projects?

We have to be willing to learn. Maybe the idea is good, but the timing is wrong. Maybe we did lose this battle (for funding, recognition, acceptance, whatever was important to us). Do we have the creative resilience to learn and move on? Can we continually take new risks rather than settling on what we want to be our laurels?

☛ WHY WE FAIL

What are the primary causes of creative failure? In *The Creative Habit*, Twyla Tharp offers a comprehensive list, saying that to "get the full benefit of failure you have to understand the reasons for it."

❶ *A failure of skill*, where your ideas exceed your skills. "If you don't have a broad base of skills, you're limiting the number of problems you can solve when trouble hits."

❷ *A failure of concept.* The solution to a weak idea? Move on.

❸ *A failure of judgment.* You listen to yourself or someone else when you shouldn't. Get wise advice, not just any advice. And learn the difference between the two.

❹ *A failure of nerve.* You aren't willing to take enough risk. You stop short of what you could and should do.

❺ *A failure through repetition.* It worked before, so do the same thing again and again…and again.

❻ *A failure from denial.* "Creating anything new and fresh is a brazen, presumptuous act…. Denial becomes a liability when you see that something is not working and you refuse to deal with it."

Failure often comes from lack of experience or lack of courage. Creating at its heart demands risk-taking. Without pushing ourselves, we won't continually learn and grow.

How best to address these common causes of failure? In building your creative life, each step in the creative process can help. Rambling and capturing your ideas in a notebook can put additional tools in your toolbox and broaden your skills. Rambling and engagement in new and different areas stretches you and helps you avoid getting stuck in a rut. By engaging and acting (digging deeper into new problems, new techniques, and new experiences), you improve your judgment and overcome your fear. Inviting others to tweak your work can help you see when denial or the ruts of repetition threaten your work; they help test your judgment and hone your skills.

In short, failure (or simply failing to be perfect) is simply another learning opportunity, not the end of your creative road.

Experiments

You should be well-immersed in your own work now—which means you'll be experimenting with your own work. Here are few reminders:

❏ *Work with the door closed* while you are learning the process. Open it to critique only when you've carried the work as far as you can on your own. (Once you have learned to work alone and what works best for your process, you can use collaboration as it suits your purpose and style.) Meanwhile, if you find it difficult to work in isolation, try working in a coffee shop where you can work alone with others around.

❏ If you haven't identified at least one critique partner or a group where you can get feedback *when you are ready to open the door,* keep looking. Finding the right person or people can take a while, but it is worth the search—even if you aren't quite ready for them yet.

Cathy Pickens

Chapter 8
Expand

"Work like hell at something just a little creative. No man grows old as long as he can create. You may die in the midst of it...but you don't die of lethargy."

Raymond Chandler, author

We all want our lives to have meaning. We want to be more than a number or a face in a homogenous crowd. That striving is universal. When I was in school, still wondering what I would major in and what I would do with my life, my mother asked me an important question, one I still ponder: "What if you find your life has no big something in it?" It's worth pondering. And "something" needs to be defined.

I've been fortunate to know famous best-selling writers as well as captains of industry—people who have had "big some-things" in their lives. I've had conversations with them and listened to them talk about their art, their lives, their work, what they wanted to be when they grew up, their search for meaning.

I've also watched scores of students as they started or switched careers, looking for what they would find fulfilling, what would give meaning to their lives, wrestling with whether their lives would have some "big something."

In those conversations, I've observed that the artists and experienced creators among them understand, perhaps better than anyone, that life is lived in the small victories, the accumulation of experiences, the opportunity to see things anew, to explore, to stretch, to grow. We each define what our "somethings" are, individual to each of us.

> "Creativity brings out our knowledge, our technical abilities, our risk taking, our feelings, our resolution to accept failure and learn from it, our willingness to put forth our best effort and our acceptance of when that effort is not good enough, our willingness to learn, our willingness to experiment, our willingness to expose ourselves to rejection, and our sheer determination to make things happen. It is quintessentially what makes us human. It gives us a glimpse into our very nature, perhaps a glimpse of God himself."
>
> R.B., workshop student

Can I Live a Creative Life?

We are back where some of you began your journey, with questions. *If I'm really creative, how can I use it? How can I incorporate artistic or scientific interests into my everyday life? How can I make a difference? How can I be more effective, productive, or valuable in my career? How does this CREATE! process help me make a difference?*

The creative process is about more than a single project. The outline of the process can also serve as a roadmap for living the creative life. While each step we've seen—capture, ramble, engage, act, and tweak—is used in developing a project, each step also outlines what artists do as they develop their expertise, as they take on increasingly challenging projects, as they grow and mature and *expand* their creative *lives*.

In particular, using a notebook to help you generate, capture, and explore ideas helps you find your own path. Improving your creative abilities will naturally expand into all areas of your life, if you allow yourself to be open enough to explore how that can happen and what that would look like for you.

The more you use your creative abilities, the more places you find where you can use them. This really is the magical part that comes after developing the habits we've explored. You can expand your creative reach even in environments that do not typically encourage creative approaches (like maybe your job?).

To expand your creative reach, though, you must pay attention to what works for you, and you must take responsibility for creating the time and the space needed to continue your development. No one will do it for you. Only you know what you require; you have to take responsibility for making it happen.

Another critical element in expanding your creative reach is deciding your end game, your goal. This may require finding a balance. Quitting your well-paying corporate job so you can pursue your artistic calling as a drummer might not end happily for you or those who depend on you. Or it might. Only you know your circumstances and responsibilities, but most successful creatives find a balance between what fulfills them and what pays the bills. Integrating the two is energizing and powerful.

☞ DO WHAT YOU LOVE? Lisa Sonora Beam, an artist, wrote in her book *The Creative Entrepreneur* about why following one path to the exclusion of another might not be fulfilling: "Lots of career counseling and business coaching starts and ends with having you identify what you enjoy doing. But without considering whether what you enjoy fully uses your gifts and adds value to the marketplace, or helps you learn how to manage your business—all you might have is a heart that can easily be broken. This might sound dramatic, but it actually takes very little to derail a creative pursuit, because it is work of the heart and soul. For those who already do the work they love, yet find the financial rewards lacking, [balance] will help to achieve alignment in this area."

To illustrate balance, Beam designed The Creative Entrepreneur Mandala. (A mandala is a circular representation of unity, wholeness, or the universe, used in Buddhist and Hindu religious art and in Jungian psychology.) On her mandala, she balanced the following:

- Heart and meaning: what you value, are passionate about;
- Managerial skills and leadership tools: what personal

tools you have or need to help you in your business or in the practical side of your creative endeavors;

- Gifts and flow: what you do easily, what absorbs you;
- Value and profitability: what you do that others would pay you to do or appreciate you being able to do for them.

She illustrates each of these as four pathways. The center, where skills, passions, practical abilities, and what others would value from us intersects, she calls the "sweet spot." That's where we use all we have to offer in a meaningful way that others will find valuable. That's where we're in balance.

I like her practical approach to the topic of living as a creative person. Parents whose children want an "arty" major in college are afraid they won't be able to support themselves. Too many of us fail to think we can do both—eat and be creative. Perhaps your greatest creative act will be to find the path that balances what you want to do and what you need to do.

> "How do you translate an understanding of your personal creative profile into the protective bubble that promotes a creative climate? Look again at the clues to what motivates, intrigues, frightens, or intimidates you. Some people need independence... some people get their most creative ideas in interchange with others."
>
> Jeff Mauzy and Richard Harriman

In the early 1600's, Dutch inventor Cornelius Drebbel was the talk of Europe. He wowed emperors and kings, including James I of England, and artists such as Bacon and Rubens and scientists such as Galileo.

Ever heard of him? Probably not. He designed microscopes, telescopes, a "magic lantern" that forecast the age of motion pictures, textile dyes (including a vivid red dye sought after by nobility and religious leaders), refrigeration, the world's first working submarine, and a massive solar collector that could have heated London. Drebbel's name should be a synonym for the phrase "ahead of his time." Famous in his day, he never profited much from his work (other than the red dye, but that was because he had family members who were better businessmen than he was). His inventions had little practical application in 17th century Europe. Professor Robert Grudin observed that "history forgot Drebbel because society has no mechanism for remembering things it does not need." At the time, society simply couldn't see much use for submarines or solar collectors.

Does that mean Drebbel's creative life was a failure? I think not, but only Drebbel could answer that for himself. Almost 400 years later, philosopher Robert Grudin and I—and maybe you—are fascinated by his accomplishments and the reach of his mind. Maybe that's a big enough something. Was that what motivated Drebbel? I would guess not. If he was motivated by what others thought of his work, wouldn't he have given up after one of his ideas failed to make his fortune?

We must each work out for ourselves what living a creative life means. The measure should be ours, not someone else's. Is it "fame" that motivates you? Or is it delight in solving problems or expressing your own vision? Again, it comes down to balance, and finding balance is the key to successfully expanding your creative life.

Experiments

Using Lisa Sonora Beam's creative mandala as a spark, I created my own to summarize the elements important in the CREATE! process (see Experiments in Chapter 4). The petals reflect what I see as the important components balanced in the process:

- ❑ Discipline and play
- ❑ Passion and risk-taking
- ❑ Divergence and connection
- ❑ Beginner and expert
- ❑ Alone and with others
- ❑ Open and focus

At the center is the concept we returned to time and again: the need for balance. The steps leading to these balanced elements are those in the CREATE process: Capture, Ramble, Engage, Act, Tweak, and Expand.

Try drawing your own mandala or mind map or roadmap or other graphic representation of what you've learned as you've explored your creative process. Take some time to thumb back through this book. What are the most important components for you? What experiments will you do next? Are you remembering to capture, cogitate, and ramble on a regular basis, to keep your well of ideas full?

Commencement:
Time to Choose

If you are off and running with your own projects, we'll say good-bye now, so you can get to work.

If you haven't done so already, choose a project in which you'll make something. What you choose isn't as important as settling on *something*. Rather than trying an updated version of the Sistine Chapel ceiling or writing your Great American Novel as your first creative act, start small. Read the instructions on your camera and start carrying it around with you, taking pictures. Talk to yourself in your notebook about how the steps you take in creating a pleasing photograph reflect the steps in the creative process.

Or pick a project around your house you've intended to tackle but you've postponed, for lack of time or fear of failure or fear it won't be perfect or for whatever reason. Find the time and the courage to tackle it.

As you travel your CREATE! path, visit cathypickens.com and share what you've discovered and what you're creating.

Whatever you choose to work on and wherever your creative path takes you, I wish you luck and happiness. May your creative path rise to meet you, and God bless.

Cathy Pickens

Appendix I:
Brain Owners' Quick-Start Guide

> One important measure of creative ability—divergent thinking skills—tests how many different ideas a person can generate in a short time. 98% of three- to five-year-olds rank at the top on divergent thinking scales. Sadly, only 2% of adults score at the top.

C an it be true that we're *born* creative and lose it? Spend only a little time around toddlers and you'll find yourself in the presence of energy and humor and make-believe. The things we later call "creative" are organic and abundant at that age.

What happens to our creative toddlers—our creative selves—as we grow up? Brain science offers part of the answer: toddlers' brains are denser than adult brains, rich environments for fresh thinking. As we mature, our capabilities are biologically narrowed, but we bring some of this loss on ourselves. Focus on "finding *the* answer" or coloring inside the lines rather than on exploring smothers our creative problem-solving ability. We do need to learn discipline and order and how to stand quietly in the lunch line, but we also need to be aware where this culturally-driven creativity drain continues into our adult work lives.

> What we have been given naturally can be tamped down or even smothered if we meet too much discouragement or too little reinforcement. Creativity researcher E. Paul Torrance found that "very young children draw transparencies in which the insides show through or show one thing behind another. However, they are taught very soon that this is not 'realistic' or 'correct,' so this kind of response quickly fades out except for a very small number of resistant children."

In most organizations—businesses as well as educational institutions—organized, coordinated, well-planned, left-brain thinking is rewarded, while artistic, free-wheeling approaches are not seen as hard-driving or profit-oriented enough to be successful. And let's face it, it's just easier to manage those who follow the well-worn, predictable paths and don't stray too far "outside the box."

The lesson? We all have innate creative abilities. For a variety of reasons, we stop using them. The good news, though, is we haven't permanently lost our abilities. But we do need to move past some myths.

> "All children are artists, and it's an indictment of our culture that so many of them lose their creativity, their unfettered imaginations, as they grow older."
>
> Madeleine L'Engle, writer

Brain Myths

Myth #1. Only geniuses are creative, and I'm no genius.

False. Given that you have enough intelligence to be competent in your field, studies show higher IQ scores are not associated with greater creative ability. And just how do you know you aren't a genius? We have more abilities than we give ourselves credit for having. In fact, developmental psychologists and brain researchers have moved away from the notion of a single "intelligence quotient" or IQ measure of smartness. Instead, most recognize "multiple intelligences."

Psychologist, author, and Harvard professor Howard Gardner identified eight "multiple intelligences" or ways in which humans can be both "smart" *and* creative:

❑ Verbal/linguistic intelligence

❑ Mathematical/logical intelligence

❑ Spatial (design) intelligence

❑ Musical intelligence

❑ Bodily/kinesthetic intelligence (dance, athletics)

❑ Intrapersonal intelligence (reflective, philosophical)

❑ Interpersonal intelligence (understand others)

❑ Naturalist intelligence (understanding the world of nature)

Rather than a short list, other researchers argue for infinite ways we can be smart. Each of us has a unique set of natural abilities, neural pathways, hormonal and other internal chemical environments, external experiences, and learned responses that we brought with us at birth and developed in life. For that reason, the number and kinds of intelligence can be as varied as humans themselves are. In other words, we are each "smart" and "creative" in our own unique way. Defined this way, the recognition of multiple intelligences says that each of us has the capacity for creativity, even though my natural abilities, as affected by my experiences, will look very different from yours.

> "Eye color essentially does not change and can be measured reasonably objectively. The same is not true of genius.... Possessing genius is much like possessing beauty—it depends on who is doing the judging."
>
> Robert Weisberg, psychologist

Having multiple ways of being "smart" means we can modify or improve our natural abilities. We are not stuck with what we have. In fact, in order to be more creative, you may need to unlearn some of the limiting notions you were taught about how to think, process information, solve problems, and respond to change in order to find what works best for you.

We all develop habits—well-worn ruts—for how we approach

life, solve problems, or deal with change. In one study, when students were asked to design a new car, they tended to rely on verbal descriptions even when a drawing or mathematical description would work better as an explanation or solution. Most of us communicate with words, either spoken or written, so words are often our default setting. But we can work to develop other parts of our repertoire, to add more tools (numbers or pictures, for instance) to our toolbox for analyzing and describing.

The more easily you can think and communicate across boundaries that others lack the training or understanding to cross, the more valuable your unique set of abilities becomes. In our globally competitive age, an advantage that is not easily duplicated by others is valuable indeed.

Expanding the experiences and databases stored in your brain allows you to draw on another evolutionary strength: the ability to learn from mistakes and to improvise in changing circumstances. According to developmental molecular biologist John Medina, when schools or employers insist on set ways of doing things, they ignore what has been one of our evolutionary strengths: the ability to improvise. Pulling only from what we already know or what easily comes to mind means we don't look for new connections or options. "Creativity suffers," Medina says.

On the other hand, we cannot rely on our ability to improvise if we lack proficiency in a subject (or in multiple subjects). Lack of knowledge limits our ability to meet challenges; we end up needlessly reinventing the wheel. This is particularly true if we lack either the skills to analyze deeply or to conceptualize broadly. In other words, we need to learn as much as we can, but we can't be limited only by what we know. We have to be willing to try new things in new ways.

We don't lose this ability to learn—or create—just because we grow older.

Thanks to its neuroplasticity, your brain can continue to reorganize and rewire itself throughout your life. Though children, of course, have an advantage, adults too can continue to deepen skills and develop new ones, to add to and improve our mental abilities. You'll reap the benefits if you're willing to put in some work.

Myth #2. Being creative looks so easy in others and feels so hard for me, so I must not be creative.

False. This is a damaging misconception about creativity. The more experienced a creative person becomes, the more familiar she is with her own creative process, and the easier the next creative project may become. Also with experience comes the understanding that tough patches are inevitable but surmountable.

> "Can people reared in the American culture accept a concept of creativity that cannot be attained instantly—a kind of creativity that requires perseverance, diligence, time, and hard work?"
>
> E. Paul Torrance

Creating never gets truly easy. Each project is different. Successful artists seek challenge. Artists want the next project to slightly exceed their grasp. The demarcation between people who create and those who don't is often not one of gift but of effort.

Few of us get to see all the decisions that led to the final product. Bantam-Doubleday executive editor Toni Burbank said, "I'm sure many readers think books all just flowed out the way the publisher printed it. It looks so perfect and final. Few people see the dozens or hundreds of sketches a designer makes, the faltering first, second, and third drafts. I used to wave around a half-inch-thick file that consisted entirely of revisions to the table of contents—names of parts and chapters, order of chapters—for a book that became a bestseller. A half-inch file! People don't believe that many revisions just for a table of contents."

☛ NEVER SATISFIED

In a study of art students, researchers Getzels and Csikszentmihalyi evaluated the students' innate creativity and their later success. The researchers found no character traits that predicted who among the students would become successful artists. Instead, what distinguished the students with the best work was how they approached their work. The best students took more time in deciding what they were going to do. At the deadline, when the students turned in their projects, the students with the best-rated work were most likely to say that it needed more work and wasn't finished.

Revisited seven years later, the best student artists—those who had examined many options and taken time before deciding to work, who were willing to change directions or start over, who evaluated more options, and who said they did not consider the work finished even when they turned it in—were also the ones who tended to be most successful in their careers.

Another distinguishing factor: Even though the successful students weren't satisfied and thought their pieces needed more work, they still delivered on time. This is an important balance to strike between constant striving toward an ideal and the realities of meeting deadlines—a balance creative people must always seek.

This study showed the differences between those who were successful artists from those who were talented enough to be admitted to art school but who weren't successful as career artists. The successful ones fully engaged in the process and did not rush to a final product. The others simply didn't work that way.

In other words, for the most successful, the secret was work, not raw talent alone.

The myth that creating is easy for others grows in part from our fascination with what's been called a cognitive snap, a precipitating event, or a "eureka" or "a-ha" moment. Stories abound of creative breakthroughs that just came to someone in a blinding flash. A sudden blindingly brilliant revelation, an a-ha moment that comes from the blue—that sounds like just the ticket. *Boy, you think, if I had one of those, I'd really be creative.* Anecdotes from the lives of artists and scientists show that those moments do occur—but story after story shows that they never occur quite the way we might hope.

The term "eureka" is attributed to Archimedes, who allegedly exclaimed "I have it!" in Greek when he realized the water level in his bathtub rose as he submerged himself. In a blinding flash, he realized the water was displaced equal to his weight, and he had the solution to a problem his mind had been wrestling with: how to prove that a crown crafted for the king was pure gold.

Much of the early research on creativity focused on creative individuals and their accounts of these kinds of groundbreaking insights. One of the most cited stories is how Friedrich von Kekulé wrestled for months to unlock the chemical structure of benzene. Then, snoozing in front of his fire, it came to him in a dream: a snake biting its tale. Eureka! A ring structure explained benzene perfectly.

These stories and others often ignore an important precursor to the a-ha. Whether in science, the arts, or business, the a-ha moment didn't pop out of a brain unbidden. In each of these famous a-ha or eureka tales, the brain had been prepared, the time put in, the work done. The Muses don't show up and crack anyone in the head with a magic wand or drop solutions down their chimney like little bundles of joy.

> "Inspiration tends to visit people who renew contact with the major challenges of some ongoing project every day and who set no time limit on their involvement."
>
> Robert Grudin, philosopher

Because some of us long for it to be easy, the "worked hard" part is often overlooked in these tales of "then brilliance struck." However, with focus and hard work as prelude, downtime can be an important ingredient. Sleeping on it or even a quick walk around the block, tackling a task that calls on another part of the brain, conferring with a colleague, or even a catnap can joggle loose pieces into place.

Is it magic? Maybe. Remember, though, the hard work comes before the nap or the walk or the bath.

Myth #3. Creativity is for artists, not people who must make a living doing practical things.

False. This myth is founded in the same ignorance and defeatism that forces children to start coloring inside the lines and painting tree leaves green instead of purple. Why would we assume that a landscape artist requires more creativity than a research scientist, a banker, or a parent raising a child? Or why assume that something beautiful isn't practical or valuable? A comfortable house designed to make people feel welcome or a quilt stitched to delight the eye as well as warm a cold night show that creativity can appear wherever creative people find themselves.

> "Creativity must be seen in the work of the scientist as well as in that of the artist...in captains of modern technology as well as in a mother's normal relationship with her child."
> Rollo May, creativity researcher and existential psychologist

Many of us put aside our creative loves because we're told, "You can't make a living doing that." True, not many people support themselves painting watercolors or writing books. Some do, but many more find ways to support themselves *and still* paint or write or sing.

Being practical and being creative are not mutually exclusive. I would argue that pursuing your creative interests and developing your own creative process will *enhance* your practical pursuits. Being passionate about writing mysteries has opened up my understanding of the power of stories, which in turn improved my work as a lawyer, a teacher, an administrator, and a volunteer. Understanding the steps in the creative process has helped me take risks, solve problems, and face setbacks, improved my ability to observe and find connections, and helped me understand that criticism is useful.

We're often encouraged to "do what you love." I love doing lots of things, but mountain clog dancing probably wouldn't keep food on my table (or pay for my knee repair surgery—clogging can be hard on the knees!). The better encouragement starts with two questions: What are you passionate about? And how can you support yourself doing it?

> "Cooking, gardening, relating with others, addressing the challenges of our occupations, teaching, waiting tables, and advancing one's business can all be creative actions. The specific nature of one's activities is not nearly as important as how they are approached."
>
> David Ulrich, photographer

A few years ago someone told me only 200 fiction writers in the U.S. support themselves with their writing. I don't know if that's accurate, but it's closer to reality than the idea that all writers are whisked from book signings to television appearances in limousines. Despite the fact that their writing doesn't pay all their bills, lots of novelists still find ways to do what they love: write novels.

The tension between passion and practicality exists in the lives of most creative people, and it requires finding a *balance* that will be different for each one. For many, it involves finding a balance between having time and having money. For me, I've discovered the need to balance my love of being alone with the reality that being around others sparks ideas. I've long dreamed of hiding in a mountain cabin with nothing to do but write. But would I be as creatively productive as a recluse? It's a question of balance.

Even the mundane can feed our creativity. We may need to balance what we think we want with the very things we think we want to avoid.

☞ "NEVER."

Nobel physicist Richard Feynman watched Princeton University reward its best scientists by freeing them from classroom teaching duties and putting them in a think tank, the Institute for Advanced Study. "These poor bastards could now sit and think clearly all by themselves, OK? So they don't get any ideas for a while: They have every opportunity to do something, and they're not getting any ideas."

After watching the "poor bastards," Feynman realized he preferred teaching. Even though answering students' questions usually wasn't much of a challenge for him, those questions sometimes led to new avenues of research by reminding him of something he hadn't returned to in a while. If nothing else, he said, he could play with new ways of getting information across to his students. "So I find that teaching and the students keep life going, and I would never accept any position in which somebody has invented a happy situation for me where I don't have to teach. Never."

Our job—whatever it is—isn't what motivates us, what gives us energy. Passion motivates us from inside, from our talents, interests, values, or sense of fun. Those who slog to work only to pay the rent and count the ticks of the clock until they can leave are *extrinsically motivated*. It's not the job that's the slog; it's how they respond to their job.

Have you seen guys dressed in goofy suits standing at the side of the road, listlessly trying to wave you into some business? Have you also seen guys dressed in similar goofy suits who seemed to be enjoying their own antics, who made you smile and maybe even wave in return? Those guys have the same jobs, but they don't have the same approach to their jobs.

Extrinsically motivated people aren't all listless and bored. Some skitter about seeking approval or recognition rather than their own satisfaction with their work. They too are looking outside themselves for motivation.

Intrinsic motivation, on the other hand, is the strongest, most durable, and most creatively productive source of motivation. For example, if someone is paid to run experiments, he may quickly tire of doing the same thing over and over again, even though it brings in a paycheck. Thomas Edison probably became frustrated as he struggled to solve a storage battery problem. But he never quit, even though it took 10,296 experiments before he found a solution. Few things better illustrate the power of intrinsic motivation—of doing something because you love it—than 10,296 experiments.

Passion can't be faked. Passion catches you unawares. Exploring your creative process increases the odds that you will stumble across what ignites your passion—or that it will find you.

Myth #4. I'm too logical and "left brain" to be creative.

In the 1970s, Nobel Laureate Roger Sperry studied epilepsy patients whose brains had been surgically split to control their seizures. Studying what the corpus callosum (the brain's traffic cop between the two sides of the cerebral cortex) controls led to the notion that some of us are "left brainers" and some of us are "right brainers." Since then, the left/right brain dichotomy has been solidified in how we think about our brains and our abilities. Most of us easily classify ourselves and others into one camp or the other. That is one of the problems. While it seems a simple, direct separation, reality is not so neat; we have limited our thinking and our creative abilities because we don't understand how our brains work.

We do have two sides to our brains. The left hemisphere of the brain processes in a linear fashion and controls our logic, sequencing ability, calculation, speech, and writing skills. The right hemisphere processes images, patterns, symbols, spatial relationships, ambiguity, and complexity.

Lots of artists consider themselves "right-brainers," while financiers and engineers are "left-brainers." But look again at those lists. Where is a writer without left-brain language skills? Or an engineer without right-brain spatial skills?

Look at the rich brains of small children. The corpus callosum doesn't start directing traffic between the two sides of the brain until we reach about age 5, which allows the two sides to develop independently. The corpus callosum does not fully separate the function of the two lobes until we reach ages 9 to 12. Not coincidentally, these ages correspond with observations about a loss of creative ability as children mature, a change that is likely enhanced by early education, socialization, and peer pressure to conform.

> "Many of us who were taught from early childhood to think linearly may actually think that inspiration should present itself to us linearly—but it just doesn't."
>
> Peggy Hadden, artist

The truth is that, absent an injury, we all have functioning bi-lobal or two-sided brains, and we can all work to develop the abilities of both sides of our brains. The dominance of one hemisphere over the other has much to do with our habits and the thought processes we fall easily into—which means those processes can be modified or relearned.

Myth #5. It's too late for me to become more creative.

False. Research indicates that brain plasticity (the ability to grow and change) continues into old age. True, some things we lose as we age; for example, a new language is most easily acquired by children, and men over 40 may not be able to learn to type. But other abilities remain the same or even improve because, as we age, we can build on experience.

The neural connections in our brains can be altered or strengthened as we use them—or abandon them. According to neurobiologist John Medina, "Researchers have shown that some regions of the adult brain stay as malleable as a baby's brain, so we can grow new connections, strengthen existing connections, and even create new neurons, allowing all of us to be lifelong learners." And lifelong creators.

When we say, "I can't learn a new language" or "I can't learn to dance," what we are really saying is "I don't want to learn that." We don't have the patience or the focus on learning new things that we had when, as toddlers, we stooped to watch ants crawl or we first began to acquire words or learn to walk.

> "There is no expedient to which a man will not go to avoid the real labor of thinking."
> Thomas Edison, inventor

The learning capacity of small children is amazing, and they do have an advantage over those of us with older brains. The reason is that, by the age of three, toddlers have two or three times the number of neural connections they will have as adults. Until about age eight, their brains remain very dense, able to make phenomenal numbers of neural connections. Then the body whips out chemical scissors and begins to lop off the neural pathways that are not being used.

Continuing over the course of our lives, though, neural pathways become stronger the more we use them, making the flow of chemical transmitters smoother. Nobel laureate Eric Kandel's research on sea snails showed that when a synapse (the connection between two neurons in the brain) fires, it causes a chemical change in the brain. By doing the same act and firing along the same pathway at least five times, it becomes easier for the firing to continue to occur in the future. This "hardening" of the neural pathway allows us to get better at something the more we do it.

Some complex tasks, such as learning to play the piano as a child, harden the pathways early and well. This may explain why so many successful violinists (or, where I'm from, "fiddle players") start as toddlers; it may also explain why my sisters and I felt forced to bribe another sister—an accomplished musician on many instruments—to please stop trying to learn the violin when she was in high school. It was just too painful to endure (and yet another example of the damaging effect peer pressure can have on creative growth!).

When we hit puberty and our teen years, another brain rewiring takes place. That strange teenage behavior attributed to hormones, those blank stares blamed on insolence, likely have more to do with the brain turning literally to mush as it rewires itself. What effect does that have on creative ability? How is it moderated by peer pressure to conform? Using fMRIs (functional MRIs or brain scans) and other technology to map the human brain's development has led to astonishing breakthroughs, but we don't have anywhere near all the answers to our nature-versus-nurture questions. We do know that brain development is diverse, variable in every person in terms of what is developed, what is pruned, and at what rate, and dependent on more than just what we were born with.

In short, we are born with a mass of traits and abilities that affect how we can be creative—and we can continue to develop new ways to be creative.

Our brain and body can be encouraged to work together. Dancers, athletes, and others talk about the importance of muscle memory and the power of visualization: how repeating an action in your mind's eye improves the body's ability to perform it. This proves useful whether the goal is to improve or learn a golf swing, a business presentation, or a dance routine. Singer/songwriter Judy Collins, as a young girl, memorized a Mozart piano concerto for a concert with the Denver symphony orchestra. She was so focused on the task that her teacher had to tell her to quit practicing so much, to skip some days. The breaks helped, she found, but on the family car trip across country, she also practiced by running her fingers along a cardboard keyboard in the back seat of the car, learning the piece in a whole new way.

☞ THE POWER OF VISUALIZATION

According to Michael Ray and Rochelle Myers, authors of *Creativity in Business,* by using the power of visualization:

- Jack Nicklaus changed his golf grip and subsequently improved his golf game by 10 strokes;

- Taffy Pergament, 1963 national novice figure-skating winner, originated a new jump, the "Taffy";

- a gynecologist discovered how to tie a surgical knot deep in the pelvis with one hand;

- Elias Howe had the crucial insight necessary for his creation of the lockstitch sewing machine;

- Louis Agassiz found a way to extract a fossil, undamaged, from a stone slab;

- H. V. Hilprecht realized how to fit certain

archaeological fragments together, enabling him to decipher their cuneiform inscriptions;

- Otto Loewi devised the experiment that led to his 1936 Nobel Prize for the discovery of the chemical basis for neural transmissions.

Unlearning or moving past the lies we've taken as truth is the first step to understanding and using our own creative abilities. Everyone has unique ability, not just a gifted few. These abilities have practical, logical uses. Developing them isn't easy for anyone, even though the end result may make it look simple. We have to exercise those skills, in the same way I have to get on the treadmill every day. The benefits are worth the effort.

Cathy Pickens

APPENDIX II
CREATE! at Work

> "Now I view creativity in two ways: first, an escape from the 'real world' and second, a way to evolve in my performance at work."
>
> J.B., workshop student

You will want to carry what you've learned about your newly developed creative skills out into a work world that may not seem welcoming. My work with business school graduate students who face that very quandary is what sparked this book. Watching them hit their creative stride even in jobs that aren't identified as "creative" has been one of the great pleasures of this journey for me.

What follows may spark ideas for bringing the artist side of your life into your work world.

The Creative Organization

Organizational leaders recognize the value of new ideas and of innovation. That's a no-brainer. What leader would say that "new and improved" is not important? But knowing how to encourage and develop that new thinking presents, for many leaders, an inscrutable mystery.

In the 1950s, academics, businesses, and the military used everything in their scientific and organizational arsenals to investigate and make the creative act routine and predictable, just as they worked to make the rest of management practice and manufacturing routine and predictable. During the post-World War II rebuilding, Japan proved fertile ground for these management ideas, which were eventually re-imported to the United States as Japan's *kaizen teian* system, which uses worker suggestions to continually improve processes. These improvement teams morphed into a multiplicity of systems that measure efficiency and quality improvement, but their track record is less encouraging when it comes to developing meaningful creativity and innovation within organizations. Part of the reason is that these suggestion systems tend to build incremental improvements on what already exists, rather than creating whole new products, systems, or ideas.

A Creative Shift

To focus on increasing creative output in organizations, business schools in the 1980s added courses on creativity, and businesses searched in earnest for the secret to improved creativity. Was it hiring creative people? If so, how to recognize them? Was it creating an environment that spawned creative thought? If so, how?

Business structure can encourage or discourage creative contributions but, at its essence, creativity is individual. Both the right people and the right environment proved to be important, but finding creative people and nurturing them proved anything but predictable—or measurable. Without predictable metrics, many companies gave up institutionalizing creativity as a bad experiment.

> "...a remarkable amount of imagination has been exercised in studying imagination, and we are none the worse for it. Alas, we are not too much wiser, either."
> Philip Johnson-Laird, psychologist

Other companies have unlocked the secret, recognizing that managing creativity requires different attitudes and reward systems than running a traditional assembly line. Even among manufacturing firms, though, the best among the assembly-line runners have discovered that expecting employees to be creative yields amazing dividends.

Organizations have trouble making this shift, though. For what management guru Peter Drucker called knowledge workers (or creative workers), you can't pay them, order them, or threaten them into bringing their whole selves to the job. As Daniel Pink has more recently emphasized in *Drive,* they are motivated from within. Developing leaders and building systems that generate passion and allow creativity to operate requires constant risk-taking and balance—a creative act all its own.

Creativity Killers

Not for lack of trying, many corporate creativity programs have failed to live up to their promise.

Why? Because institutions—of any kind or size—are better at killing creativity than encouraging it. Harvard professor Teresa Amabile's September 1998 *Harvard Business Review* article "How to Kill Creativity" provided a title that has sparked lively discussion in countless corporate workshops. Just like most humans, most organizations—not just businesses, but not-for-profits and governmental agencies, not just large but small ones, too—prefer order to chaos, sure things to risky ones, people who do as they're told to those who aren't predictable.

For those reasons, organizations often pay little more than lip-service to creativity programs. Anyone who has spent time in an organization can outline the leadership and organizational traits that kill creativity.

Leaders set the tone for the level of creativity in an organization, just as they set the tone for other aspects of an organization. According to Gerd Gigerenzer, the German psychologist whose research was popularized in Malcolm Gladwell's bestseller *Blink*, "These rules tend to become absorbed into the organizational bloodstream, where they may linger long after the leader has moved on.... A leader who appears suspicious of employee absences discourages people from going to conferences or considering outside educational opportunities. Employees may be grateful that such shortcuts help them avoid protracted mulling over the pros and cons of taking a particular course of action. But as everyone adopts the same rules, the culture shifts: becoming more or less open, more or less inclusive, more or less formal. Because

Cathy Pickens

such behavior is difficult to change, leaders should think carefully about what values their rules communicate."

Creatives abandon organizations or leaders who have rules against wandering too close to the edge of the box. Even though most organizations and leaders are not openly hostile, they may be benignly neglectful—or afraid. Most leaders don't set out to kill creativity, but their fear of other things (such as losing control, losing face, failing, looking bad to their bosses) prompts behavior that kills creativity.

☞ COMMON CREATIVITY-KILLING LEADER BEHAVIORS

- Tight controls on employee time and discretion, often borne of suspicions that employees aren't working hard enough and may be wasting time, or that employees don't have the information or motivation to do tasks without close supervision.

- Too much focus on outcomes rather than efforts and on short-term results rather than the longer term.

- A "winner's win" or "we succeed" mentality, which can have the unintended consequence of stifling even modest risk-taking. If the culture focuses only on winning, who would risk even a modest failure?

- No understanding of the creative process—the value of rambling, of separating idea generation from evaluation, of matching skills and offering challenges, of trial and error and re-visioning a project.

- Ordering employees to "be creative" or "think outside the box" with no support for new ideas, no assurance of protection for risk-taking, and no clear fit between that "outside the box" mandate and the corporate culture.

- No understanding of the long-range view needed for real innovation.

> "No professional field, no matter how enthusiastically it endorses innovation, is free from a nagging and purely self-interested resentment of newness."
> Robert Grudin, philosopher

At its heart, the reason leaders hold creative efforts at arm's length—or actively oppose them—is fear. To put it bluntly: "The hardest part of being creative is that it is very threatening to those who are not," said artificial intelligence specialist Roger Schank. As a result, "large corporations attract the least creative people who can do the job." After all, it's easier to do the job if the boat isn't rocking.

> "Soviet scientists and engineers were acknowledged to be among the best and most creative in the world.... A bad system will beat a good person every time."
> Alan Robinson and Sam Stern, management experts

Can we structure an organization that can overcome these drawbacks? Absolutely. In fact, even when the most creative, capable minds are available, it is imperative to have a system that avoids *structural creativity killers*.

☞ STRUCTURAL CREATIVITY KILLERS

- Focus on procedures, politics, immediate profitability, and career advancement to the exclusion of longer-term, more creatively productive goals.

- Organizational silos or strict hierarchies that prevent information, resources, ideas, and needs from flowing easily between divisions or levels.

- A system that pays employees for ideas. Rewarding employees for new ideas, at first glance, looks like a good plan, but a reward yields what is rewarded. In the case of money for ideas, it means employees will spend less time exploring and moving beyond the obvious so they can move straight toward the reward. Employees aren't stupid. Psychologist Edward Deci agrees: "In fact, money may work to 'buy off' one's intrinsic motivation for an activity." Decades of motivation research has shown that money doesn't motivate; passion and personal investment do.

- Hiring employees specifically to be creative. Again, this seems counterintuitive, but a study cited by Thomas Lockwood and Thomas Walton in *Corporate Creativity* shows that "groups of new employees, hired to be more creative than existing ones, eventually stopped using their creative abilities and come to resemble their less creative counterparts. Why?... As the new employees brought fresh thinking into the establishment, they threatened the established norms. In order to protect those norms, other employees brought increasing levels of judgment to bear on the new ideas until they brought the 'creative' group into line with the existing organization. Much, but not all, of the change wrought in the more creative group was found to occur through attrition." In other words, the ones hired to be creative became dissatisfied because of the peer pressure and left.

Even though developing individual and organizational creativity is an indisputable benefit, I'm not a big fan of most corporate creativity programs for one simple reason: most of them ignore what artists know about the creative process. So what's an organization to do?

A Few Ways to Save Creativity in Organizations

Just as leadership and organizational traits can kill creativity, they can also provide a safe harbor to encourage creativity and innovation.

One of the first questions a manager must ask is, "Why would my employees bother going outside their normal job responsibilities to bring new ideas to the table?" Employees have "discretionary energy," something beyond what they are paid for doing but which they can voluntarily bring to the job. Why would they freely offer part of themselves to an employer?

In some organizations, new ideas, innovation, and change are not welcomed. We have watched many of these organizations fail, though some continue to plod along. Even though the party line in most organizations is that good new ideas are welcomed, individual leaders within those organizations may be reluctant to commit time or resources to explore and develop those ideas—for fear of their own survival.

As counterpoint, the legends around companies such as 3M, Hallmark, and Google set the bar for how to structure creative time within a company. For example, they allow employees unstructured time to explore and develop promising ideas (3M's famous skunk works, where individual development time led to Post-It Notes, among other inventions, or Google's "20% time," where employees were encouraged to work on their own ideas on company time) or provide sabbaticals for employees to investigate and get ideas from other fields (Hallmark). These systems are based in what artists know about the creative process—that capturing, cogitating, and rambling are the first steps. And it can work.

From the best companies, we know it is possible to build creative processes into an organization. From all those companies who've tried and failed, we also know it's difficult.

An unexpected example of a constantly innovating culture can be found in a staid heavy industry: Nucor Steel, the largest U.S. steel producer and steel recycler. Employees on the manufacturing floor at Nucor are immersed in a culture that's always looking for faster and better. Hanging out with people who believe that things can always be better, who are passionate about new ideas, who ask "what if?" and "I wonder?" and other door-opening questions creates a contagious environment.

Visitors to Nucor plants marvel that their machinery has productivity yields multiple times higher than the machines are rated to produce. Former CEO Ken Iverson said visitors always wanted to know who made Nucor's machinery, but he pointed out the secret wasn't the machinery; the secret was Nucor's workforce. The Nucor website announced, "For us, research and development isn't a department, it's a way of life."

But how is an environment like that established and maintained? At Nucor, employee bonuses were closely tied to clear metrics; everyone from the receptionist at the front door to the employee loading steel trusses on a truck could tell you the plant's annual goal for quality tons of steel produced safely—and by how much they think they can exceed that goal. This is an important distinction: Nucor didn't pay people for ideas; Nucor paid the entire team for increases in productivity. Rather than offering money (an extrinsic reward), Nucor activated employees' sense of involvement and called on their discretionary energy. Their *focus* on uniformly held goals and values was important.

Nucor's leadership style and structure offers several lessons on calling out this intrinsic motivation or discretionary energy:

- Employees must know their jobs are important—and *how* they are important. They need to see the complete project and how they fit into it. At Nucor, even the maintenance staff shared in the plant's productivity bonuses because everyone played a role in each plant's success or failure.

- Employees need to understand the corporate culture, the mission, the company's brand, and its values. How do you know whether your company is doing this? Look at what gets talked about and what commands the most time and money. How do employees and customers describe your organization?

- Employees need continual feedback on their performance. Nucor typically paid below-market wages but offered an aggressive bonus plan based on team performance. It also helped that the metrics were clear, and that the bonuses were paid in each paycheck, not far removed from the performance in an annual review. In the best systems, employees should be encouraged (and able) to gather feedback themselves, from their co-workers or customers or the task itself, in order to continually improve.

- Like any artist, employees need the freedom to use their own discretion about how to solve problems. Nucor traditionally looked for workers from rural backgrounds who knew how to work with their hands and how to reason through mechanical problems.

Not all organizations can develop clear metrics as measurable as "quality tons of steel produced safely." But what do you get if you find ways to unlock the creative potential of your employees and let each one know she is important to the company's success and profitability?

Nucor Steel won an environmental award in an unpredictable way. Sludge waste had to be mixed with clay to absorb the moisture and stabilize it before the landfill would accept it. The dump truck driver knew the cost of each load depended on its weight, and more clay meant more weight. He happened to arrive at the dump one day with another waste truck driver from a nearby diaper manufacturing plant, there to dump diaper dust (the leftover material from the highly absorbent linings of disposable diapers). The light bulb went off: Instead of using heavy clay, why not mix in the lightweight diaper dust, which would end up in the dump anyway, to absorb the fluid?

Would Nucor have had the benefit of this truck driver's creativity if he hadn't known what went into making Nucor profitable and if he hadn't known the plant's managers would listen to his idea? How many companies miss out on similar light bulb moments because leaders are quick with the trigger at shooting down bad ideas but, in the process, kill a lot of good ideas?

Leaders who want to protect and encourage creativity need to recognize their job is to turn potential into performance. To do this, they need to:

- Stretch employees with challenges; give them opportunities to learn new skills, whether through workshops, education, cross-training, or rotation. Call on all the skills and talents employees bring, not just a narrow range of abilities.

- Allow employees to use their discretion whenever possible—in choosing the projects they feel best match their skills and interests and in choosing how to perform those tasks. Allow them time for "unofficial activity," to explore and think and experiment. Experience supports this: "Companies that maintain higher levels of unofficial activity tend to make better decisions," according to observations by researchers Robinson and Stern.

- Provide for diverse viewpoints; many new ideas and innovations come from combinations of visions from seemingly disparate fields. Move people around; expose them to other approaches and new fields, both inside and outside the company, inside and outside their discipline.

- Provide feedback. Better yet, design systems that allow them to gather their own feedback from their users or customers or colleagues. In providing feedback as a manager, ask "What would make this better?" or "Why do you think this went off track?" rather than "Why did you fail?"

> Concrete feedback is difficult to generate for many jobs because outcomes are not clearly measurable. Psychologist Mihalyi Csikszentmihalyi summarized the difficulty: "In the past a craftsman—whether a shoemaker, carpenter, or weaver—was able to see the object of his labors taking shape before his eyes.... It is hard to get deeply involved in an activity where one's performance is a minor factor, where a good job is scarcely noticed, and where even the worker can't determine whether his work was well done."

- Have fun. Recognize and celebrate successes—even small, incremental ones. Gather and spread stories about employees' initiatives. Be a cheerleader.

- Allow smart, calculated risks. Recognize that failures will occur when people stretch themselves. Failure frightens some businesses so much that they try to avoid it at all costs. But fear of failure by both employees and managers stifles more potentially creative work in organizations than anything else.

- Failure of some kind is inevitable. Would you rather fail because you took a risk that might have yielded benefits? Or would you rather fail by getting beat out by companies who understand what supports creative acts and are willing to turn their employees loose? Guess which failure will cost you the most in the long run.

- Be comfortable with ambiguity and conflict. As Lee Iacocca said, "Only the boss can set a tone that lets people feel comfortable enough to say those magic words, 'I don't know.'"

- Remember that idea generation and evaluation are two separate steps in the creative process. Limit criticism—of yourself and of others. Evaluating too quickly shuts down new ideas and prevents the opportunity to build on what, at first, was a weak idea.

- Be flexible. The best idea will be the one no one anticipated. If it was obvious, someone would have already done it.

- Recognize the long-term nature of creative enterprise. Sam Borenstein of Citibank said, "Innovation takes three to five years to prove itself. You need to give yourself at least that much time or you will ultimately fail." Is it always three to five years? No, but neither are results always delivered in time for quarterly financial reports. Continuing to dig in a dry hole is futile, but so is stopping short of hitting the gusher because you didn't have enough patience. Discernment and skill and calculated risk-taking are required.

- Develop a culture where everyone is involved and everyone is expected to be creative, rather than a few isolated "creative types." The companies that have the most creativity and innovation are those that expect creative acts.

As Robinson and Stern observed, "Nobody can predict *who* will be involved in them, *what* they will be, *when* they will occur, or *how* they will happen." Refusing to look for it or expect it guarantees no one will bring it.

- Offer problem-solving training. Research shows that training in creative problem-solving techniques improves scores on measures of creativity and can also be traced to better business performance.

- Carefully develop rewards. Money can be a disincentive to creative thinking because it can demean or distract from intrinsic motivation. The value of rewards will vary according to someone's age, experience, and personal values. Don't underestimate the power that recognition and autonomy have for creators.

In summary, research and experience show creativity and innovation thrive where there is "a balance of structure, or process, and autonomy; of boundaries and expansive thinking; of active management and self-direction; of homogeneity and diversity."

This need for balancing between divergent ends of several continuums illustrates why developing and maintaining a culture that nurtures creativity is so difficult. If a creative environment could be built by following a set of rules, more organizations would do it. Unfortunately, many of the rules are in conflict. The secret continues to be *balance*. Close your eyes and see how long you can stand on one leg. Balance isn't something you achieve once and check it off your list; it is a constant process of adjustment and accommodation. Again, if it was easy, everyone would do it.

Creating Inside an Organization

How do you become more creative in your business or professional life? The odds would seem insurmountably stacked against success, thanks to bureaucracy and its penchant for managing appearances, its aversion to risk, affinity for tried-and-true paths, and lack of understanding—even suspicion—of those who stick their necks out or who do things in unorthodox ways.

If you want to use your creative abilities in your work life, the easiest way is to find one of those businesses that cultivate and reward creativity. Some are large, some are small. Some are staid industries and therefore unexpected homes for creative acts. Some are started by entrepreneurs who didn't find the opportunities they craved within existing organizations. Some creative environments are open, with game tables and shared space and lively interaction, places that appeal to extroverts but where an introvert would be forced to crawl under the desk and hide. Finding an environment that feeds your creative process is important. What are the characteristics? Organizations with relaxed or flat hierarchies are good bets, as are those that seek meaningful input from employees.

In business, you should also seek creative mentors and locate yourself in a creative part of an organization. That doesn't necessarily mean in the advertising department or in an art gallery. Creative bosses exist everywhere; you just have to find them. And you have to protect yourself and your creative abilities from those who would try to stamp out any signs of creativity, usually for fear that it breeds anarchy and the next thing you know, people will be dancing, enjoying their work, or (gasp) coming up with new ideas.

Kaizen teian sounds like the ideal work situation.

Unfortunately, a name or a "team" doesn't guarantee a creative environment any more than a code of conduct guarantees an ethical company. Talk to the people who work there and observe for yourself what really happens in the organization or work group, not what upper management hopes is happening.

Though you want an organizational structure that encourages and protects creative initiative, you don't have to—and probably won't—find the perfect organization. Despite the difficulties, those who understand their own creative process are better equipped to find ways to use their abilities within an organization, no matter its structure.

In most large, bureaucratic organizations, that is exactly what must happen: you must find ways to use your process to sell your ideas, to attract resources and support within the existing political climate. Seldom does a boss show up offering boundless time and resources for you to explore and follow your passion. Maybe it happens—but rarely. And the offers are made to those who have already proven themselves as idea producers and innovators, so you can't just sit around and hope what you need will appear.

Obviously, one of the first steps is to recognize what you need. No matter the organization or its commitment to nurturing creativity and innovation, you must understand your own creative process, what motivates you, what you value, your goals, your most productive work style and rhythms. For many, it starts with being able to carve out even small blocks of time to think. For others, it requires a group to bounce ideas around with or the input of someone in a different technical specialty.

Whatever you need, you can't rely on an organization or a boss to supply it. Learning to negotiate for the right to work on something that intrigues you, to attract resources for developing or implementing ideas, and the permission (within reasonable limits) to fail should be approached as a creative exercise in its own right.

Many of us find no structure to support us. Frankly, that may be the most interesting environment in which to find your creative path. In most cases, the time, the authority, and the resources won't be handed to you—nor should it. Face it, would you be happy if it was? Most of us want to choose our projects. Making space and finding resources is what a weekend painter or a midnight writer must do. Your creative work life within an organization will likely face the same challenges of finding time and resources—and can be strengthened by the search.

Selling Your Ideas

Creativity crushers abound in the workplace, just as they do at home or at school or anywhere else. Some of the creativity crushers are of our own making: we don't do our homework, we don't consider issues or our ideas from the decision-maker's perspective, we take "no" for the answer and give up.

Bosses and co-workers do exist who lack the emotional maturity to support others' initiatives. Plenty of books have been written on toxic or stunted people and how to work with them or around them. If you can't creatively work with it, you should find a creative way out and into something else.

Many who work within organizations often complain their ideas get shot down and no one is willing to stick his head above the cubicle walls. Developing your own creative process doesn't automatically solve those problems.

You need to develop the political savvy to understand the organizational culture and the needs and motivations of those who can help you make things happen. Put yourself in the decision-maker's head. What would you want to know about a new idea? What groundwork would help convince you? What are your needs, as boss or colleague? What are your worries?

Equally important, how does the person to whom you are presenting your ideas prefer to gather information? Does she respond best to data? Does he prefer a short summary with details confined to appendices? A verbal summary? Bullet points?

If you find your ideas continually squelched, get some advice about what techniques might work better in your environment. Watch what works for others—and what doesn't.

Identify the opinion leaders and seek their input in private. Listen to them and use their recommendations to strengthen your proposal. Don't be anxious to grab credit for yourself. Ideas move faster with lots of legs carrying them.

Remember too that persistence pays. Use some judgment—don't continue trying to cross the finish line on a horse that's come up lame. But "no" or "not for us" sometimes just means "not now." Sometimes the idea has to lie fallow for a while before it's ready to produce something. Reconfigure it; time its reintroduction carefully, but don't let an idea you and others truly believe in disappear too easily.

If you've done your homework, studied the organizational culture and dynamics, anticipated the boss's needs, worries, and concerns, and you still face a stone wall, you may have to face a difficult truth: you might need to look elsewhere for your creative fulfillment—or for your paycheck. If you want to use more of your creative skills at work, you may need to find somewhere else to work, whether in another department in your current company or another organization entirely. Make sure, before you make the leap, that your ideas will find a more welcoming home.

Remember, you'll have similar challenges in selling your ideas no matter where you are.

At least now, when you go job-hunting, you'll know better what meets your needs and feeds your creativity. This time, you'll know how to use your creative skills in plotting the path to your best work situation.

Managing Creativity

No manager wants people rambling about doing things that have nothing to do with the business or sinking resources into something that will not yield a return for the organization. At the same time, the best managers recognize that the best ideas may not come from a formal process.

In any organization, just wanting new ideas isn't enough. The structure needs to encourage—or at least not squelch—the development of ideas. One CEO hired my colleagues and me for advice about why he wasn't seeing creative approaches from his executives. "I need my leadership team to start thinking outside the box!" The company had money to spend on acquisitions or new ventures, but the executive team had not come up with workable ideas about what to do with those funds.

The executive team—maybe a dozen people—gathered with us in a large room to brainstorm. Most of the executive team had been with the company for many years, often in several capacities. One new kid had been with the company for only a few months.

I looked around the room, certain the top executives must be excited about the new direction this young, diverse, highly successful company would be taking. I had to admit, they didn't look too excited. But they would be, I was sure.

When the CEO said, "I want new, out-of-the-box thinking," the first new idea came from the youngest member of the executive team, a tall, lanky guy who leaned forward in his seat, obviously energized that the team was willing to move outside its comfort zone. He offered up a second new idea, then a third, several of them quite good.

The only other person who responded was the CEO. As each new idea rose like a bright balloon, the CEO beat it into oblivion. He didn't pop it with a sharp, strategic pin. He cudgeled it into submission, then stomped it, just to make sure.

"We've tried that, that won't work." "You call that new?" "We'd lose our shirts if we invested in something like that."

After every idea the new guy suggested, the CEO revved his imaginary chainsaw and chopped him off at the knees. The new guy's enthusiasm lasted longer during that session than I expected. It certainly lasted longer than mine did. His career with the company didn't last long, though; he took his enthusiasm and ideas to a new job within a few months.

The other executives in the room knew from experience what would greet new ideas, so they saved their collective breath. As I worked with this organization, I saw what I often see in venues that at first appear arid: Lots of bright, talented, passionate people work there. In those organizations that succeed, the creative ones learn how to feed their ideas and find their way around the barriers—even when the biggest barrier is their boss. One executive at this company later told me, "The first response from the CEO is always no, always negative. But if you've shown him you've thought through how to pay for it and the expected returns, he'll be willing to listen later. I haven't had him fail to sign on for a well-researched idea. You just need to know how he works."

That's true for every organization; you just need to know how it works. That's also why that organization had been able to attract and retain talented, passionate people. Imagine, though, if the CEO wasn't someone who came back wanting to hear more. He'd soon never hear anything, because the bright, passionate ones would go elsewhere, leaving only the lumpen ones willing to slog along for a paycheck. On the downside, even those who understand how he works will carefully calculate the risks they're willing to take and will make only the safest, most defensible bets.

How ideas are evaluated affects how much risk we are willing to accept. One of the deadliest threats to creativity and innovation within an organization is harsh or premature criticism.

To be effective, leaders have learned to move quickly to assess ideas, make choices, and move. Hugh McColl, the CEO who grew Bank of America into the second-largest bank in the U.S., observed, "The ability to evaluate ideas, discard quickly those that won't work, and bet on the right horses is what has made most of us successful as leaders. That's what's gotten us where we are in an organization." But that may work against encouraging creative thinking. Slowing down, listening, reserving judgment, and letting ideas grow are techniques that must be consciously developed. As McColl points out, that may mean tamping down some of the instincts that have driven a successful executive career.

The source of our quickness to judge is hard to pinpoint. Brenda Ueland called it "that Great Murderer of the Imagination—a world of unceasing, unkind, dinky, prissy Criticalness."

Perhaps it grows from our classroom experiences or it is part of the competitive nature of business today, but much time is focused on what's wrong with an idea and picking it to pieces, and little time is spent on what is good about it.

> "Many hotshot students have been convinced that it is a mark of brilliance to find the first flaw in an argument and go for the jugular.... Our university system teaches that ideas are either right or wrong."
>
> Roger Schank, artificial intelligence researcher

Of course, many businesses have failed because decision-makers gathered in rooms and convinced each other their ideas were flawless in both conception and execution. Leaders who only want to hear good news can bring a company down quickly because those who see the emperor wandering around naked are loathe to point it out.

On the other hand, businesses can also fail, or at least fail to thrive, because they cut off good ideas without exploring them. Corporate cultures that either (1) reject ideas out of hand because taking pot-shots is easier than developing something new, *or* (2) nod everything the boss suggests into existence because no one wants to deliver bad news, are equally dangerous and short-lived. We're back to that familiar concept: *balance*.

Allowing free-wheeling thinking can be scary in any organization. In large ones, reputations and egos are at stake. For a small organization, its very survival may be on the line. New ideas should challenge the status quo, but that can also threaten job security or status. The more layers that must be sold on an idea, the less likely it will progress, not because it isn't a good idea but because it threatens someone's authority or presents too much risk for higher-ups.

How can you incorporate the benefits of a critique group into a work setting? The organizations that do it best tend to be those with research and development or marketing or communications departments where an open exchange of ideas is part of the DNA of those hired to work there. [For a look behind the curtain at one such company, read *Creativity Inc.* by Ed Catmull, one of Pixar's founders.] In other instances, managers build it into their staff meetings, where individuals feel free to bring up new ideas or problems and bat them around. That is relatively rare, but it need not be.

A trickier kind of group is one where the members are from different companies but want a place to brainstorm ideas, collaborate on a project, or hone their skills. When proprietary or competitive information is involved, these groups are risky and probably should be avoided. But I've seen one inter-company group work quite well. Some MBA students and alums from the McColl School of Business at Queens University of Charlotte had been invigorated by dynamic class discussions, so they set up a group to continue to exercise their problem-solving and creative skills. The two "founders" issued invitations, the group settled into a dozen members, and they began meeting twice a month at 7:00 a.m.—a time designed to discourage those who just wanted a social club.

They served as a sounding board for small projects presented by group members; they researched and wrote an award-winning business case on a massive public-private community initiative; and they offered their services to emerging businesses and not-for-profits as a sounding board. Their energy and commitment continued for more than a year, and they offered a range of skills and perspectives to clients and to each other, while keeping their own creative skills honed in the process, before they moved on to their own projects. Groups need not last forever to be effective.

Corporate dynamics are beyond the scope of this book. We have enough to do just managing our own tendency to criticize and condemn ideas. But we need to acknowledge that managing creative people is difficult. They challenge the orthodoxy. They head in unexpected directions. They don't always respond to money or status as rewards. They identify with and are motivated by their ideas and the challenge of the work.

So how should a leader manage creative employees (which ideally would be all of her employees) to get the most and the best for the organization without things running amok?

- Decide what is not negotiable. This may include deadlines or the reputation of the organization. Make sure everyone understands the core values, the brand, the mission of the organization, and make sure those fundamentals are shared by everyone.

- Check your tendency to evaluate and discard too quickly. To keep you honest, have an associate (someone comfortable telling you when you are naked) who will monitor you; arrange a secret signal for those times when you revert to your critical default setting.

- The most important secret is simple: Find the good parts of an idea first and commend those. Always start with positive comments. Always. The rule is simple but not always easy to remember.

- Identify the rewards an individual or group values. Not all motivations are the same; neither are all rewards.

☞ CIRQUE DU SOLEIL

> At Cirque du Soleil, makeup helps create the characters for the audience. Each performer must learn to apply his own makeup every night. "The fact that most of them were trained as athletes makes them impatient with makeup, but we've made their background work to our advantage," said Claudia, Cirque du Soleil's head makeup designer. "They are, after all, competitive. They like to be measured, to be recognized. So a few years ago I started arriving with special brushes engraved with lines like 'Best Makeup,' 'Most Improved,' 'Best Shading,' 'Best Eyes,' and so on. They love it! We want our artists to become interested in the process, because 'just following the book' is not enough."

As we have seen, professional artists tend to be accustomed to critique or feedback. Most are harder on themselves than anyone else could be. Artists are testaments that the more feedback someone receives the better she will be at receiving it. Business professor Leonard Glick agrees that "most people develop a skill of accepting feedback if they receive enough of it. If feedback is ubiquitous, each occasion is not as big a deal as when it is given annually."

Artists can teach us how to build "ubiquitous feedback" into our organizations and into how we manage creativity. In live theater, for example, the director typically ends the day's rehearsal by giving the cast and crew "director's notes," dissecting the performance and outlining what should be changed. Charina, one of Cirque du Soleil's artistic directors, gives "notes after each show about little things I noticed—what worked, what didn't, what's coming along. That way, they know I'm paying attention and their work matters. And I've learned not to give only negative notes. If you do that, after a while, whenever you give them a note, they just groan! So it's important to be positive, too."

She takes the feedback a step further and gives performers tickets to the show for those nights when they aren't performing. In her words, "the best thing I've done…is to help them see their work through the eyes of the audience…. After just one night in the audience, the artists themselves are transformed."

Professional performers are accustomed to a director's notes, but they have also had the audience's applause to buoy their egos, something unique to performers. Managers need to be cautious about implementing an artist-style critique too quickly. It takes time, skill, and care to build critique into an organizational culture, and critique can offer more harm than benefit to those who aren't experienced with this type of feedback—and who don't get to hear any applause.

In particular, when the creative act is something that has been very public and has taken a long time to put together, such as a public event or major presentation, the sense of risk and the emotional entanglement is heightened. Too often, I have watched managers leap to the critique, the preparation for "next time" with their "director's notes" when they should take time to celebrate the success and acknowledge the intense effort that went into pulling off a major event. Those who invested themselves—and their discretionary energies—into making it a success are already critiquing themselves. They don't need their boss's "help" right in the midst of their exhaustion and relief at the end of a performance. I don't know any directors who call the cast together after an opening night to crack down on their mistakes. Save your "director's notes" for the preparation phase of the next event, not the celebration phase of this one.

For those used to receiving critique or feedback, it is hard to remember the need to care for and nurture tender buds not quite ready for the strengthening wind or sharp, feeding rain. Sometimes the feedback comes unbidden or at a bad time. For those trying to encourage creative first steps, it's important to remember to hold back, to think about the real aim. Is it the finished product? Or is it the *process?*

Photographer David Ulrich points out that critique requires its own balanced creativity: "In giving feedback...it is not enough merely to be supportive. We must be honest. We must aspire to elevate our responses to the level of a creative act, looking deeply within to discover what is evoked by viewing another's efforts and giving support or due criticism where needed. We can employ our intuitive capacity and synthesize our response to another's work, to know when to uphold, when to challenge, and when to stand back and merely observe. In short, we must be willing to give of ourselves and avoid the routine formula, the easy answer."

Keep in mind where you and those around you are in the creative process. At the idea generation stage, when the group is cogitating or rambling, be more open to oddball ideas that can lead to something truly new. The farther along the creative path you are, the more structured the feedback can be.

At the same time, strike a balance; you don't want to discourage ideas, but you must also evaluate them. A creative environment does not mean no feedback, no opportunity to grow and learn, no testing, no reality-check. Instead, a creative environment demands critique.

How does this translate into a business setting? Understanding how quickly a critical word spoken too soon kills ideas could revolutionize most companies, just as training people how to use constructive critique could drive better decisions. Businesses need what artists know, but the lessons don't come in prepackaged quick doses on PowerPoint slides. The creative process must be experienced fully and over a period of time, which is why so few individuals and companies have attempted it.

But you understand the process because you've developed your own. What better business advantage than being able to develop your ideas as well as help others develop theirs?

Cathy Pickens

Endnotes

Chapter 2

12   **"... one of the dirtiest temptations."** L'Engle, *Walking On Water*, 153.

Chapter 3

15   **"... we must fix it on paper."** Dimnet, *The Art of Thinking*, 166.

18   **"Catch everything."** Bach, in Clark, *The Basics of Writing Bestsellers*, 23.

18   **"...cease to have any."** Woolf, in Romesburg, *The Life of the Creative Spirit*, 111.

18   **"...sporadic visitings of creativity."** Mallon, *A Book of One's Own*, 153.

19   **"...speed one on one's way."** Mansfield, in Johnson, *The Hidden Writer*, 144.

19   **"...ideas are already flowing."** Oldach, *Creativity for Graphic Designers*, 44.

20   **...to develop a new habit.** Lally, et al., "How Habits are Formed."

25   **"...an immediacy by hand."** Aldrich, *Notes from Myself*, 60.

25 **...imagination can cavort at will."** Grafton, "The Use of the Journal in a Private Eye Novel," 44.

29 **"...private fragmentary scribble book."** Holzer, *A Walk Between Heaven and Earth*, 38.

31 **"...feel uneasy and guilty."** Ueland, *If You Want to Write*, 38.

34 **"...doubt-impeded, ego-inflated."** Ueland, 140.

35 **"...something important to say."** Ueland, 177.

42 **"Hugely, hugely important."** Csikszentmihalyi, *Good Business*, 188. (Because I know you want to know: it's pronounced *Chik-sent-me-hi*.)

46 **"...taking care of a family."** Rainer, *The New Diary*, 294-95.

48 **"...context of your life."** Rainer, 18-19. Ellipses included in original.

Chapter 4

53 **"...from being locked in."** Halmos, in Romesburg, 136.

55 **"...challenges of our work."** Stefik & Stefik, in Lockwood and Walton, *Corporate Creativity*, 25.

56 **"...new is most important."** Collins, *Morning, Noon, and Night*, 76.

58 **"...populations like our own."** Medina, *Brain Rules*, 2.

58 **"...solve a new problem."** Medina, 14.

58 **"...a step at a time."** Johnson, in Barron, Montuori, and Barron, *Creators on Creating*, 59.

59 **"...to get recharged."** Ueland, 42.

60 **"...to live at all."** Galsworthy, in Romesburg, 274.

62 **"...over the classical arts."** Tharp, *The Creative Habit*, 74.

64 "...design more engaging." Mauzy and Harriman, *Creativity Inc.,* 19-20, 26.

66 "...anxiety-free creativity." Beam, *Creative Entrepreneur,* 40.

66 "...any taste for." Fitzgerald, in Romesburg, 219.

66 "...worthy of note." Stravinsky, in Barron, Montuori, and Barron, 192.

67 "...people were wearing." Wakefield, *Creating from the Spirit,* 241.

68 "...the right direction." Audette, *The Blank Canvas,* 51.

68 "...innocence of the eye." Ruskin, *The Elements of Drawing,* 6.

69 "...systematic practice." Stanislavski, *An Actor Prepares,* 87.

69 "...finer, and deeper." Stanisklavski, 86.

70 "...sign of ignorance." Adams, *The Care and Feeding of Ideas,* 178.

71 "...to undertake another." Hazlitt, in May, *The Courage to Create,* 66.

75 "...for us and in us." May, 66.

75 "...she could help it." May, 66.

76 "...and gently shine." Ueland, 29.

77 "...amare, to love." Cameron, *Walking in this World,* 85.

77 "...it no longer applies." Robinson and Stern, *Corporate Creativity,* 25-27.

79 "...something totally different." Mullis, in Barron, 73.

80 "...by a sculptor." Zelinski, *The Joy of Thinking Big,* 13.

80 "...painful winning of skills." Grudin, *The Grace of Great Things,* 11.

81   "...scientific fields outside his own." Block, *The Wizard of Berkeley.*

81   "...for novel problems." Stefik and Stefik, in Lockwood and Walton, 21.

82   "...turn into mastery." Barron, Montuori, and Barron, 172.

Chapter 5

98   "...your responsibility." Hadden, *The Artist's Quest of Inspiration,* 19.

99   "...experience this difficulty." Torrance, *The Search for Satori and Creativity,* 32.

99   "...in a nutshell." Tharp, 7.

99   "No explanation required." Tharp, 171.

101   "...sudden flash of enlightenment." Torrance, ix.

101   "...write a lot." King, *On Writing,* 151.

103   "...dinner bell rang." Hadden, 221.

104   "...could avoid distractions." King, 100.

105   "...undisciplined free time." Ray and Myers, *Creativity in Business,* 141.

106   "...worry a whole day." Dickens, *Letters of Charles Dickens, Vol. 2,* 6.

107   "...survives without practice." Barron, Montuori, and Barron, 171.

108   "...your mouth a liar." Pickard and Lott, *Seven Steps on the Writer's Path,* 153.

108   "...throw away the bad ones." See http://paulingblog/ wordpress.com/2008/10/28/clarifying-three-widespread-quotes. Pauling's reply is often misquoted as: "The best way

to have good ideas is to have lots of ideas and throw away the bad ones."

109 **"...limit on their involvement."** Grudin, 13.

110 **"...the substance itself."** See Shelley, Mary. Introduction to 1831 edition of *Frankenstein,* http://www.rc.umd.edu/editions/frankenstein/1831v1/intro.html.

110 **"I doubt it."** Chaplin, in Romesburg, 211.

111 **"...the rest as possible."** Lowell, in Ghiselin, *The Creative Process,* 110-11.

112 **"...to get out at."** Lowell, in Ghiselin, 111.

113 **"...volume in his head."** Root-Bernstein and Root-Bernstein, *Sparks of Genius,* 50-51.

113 **"...mind at that moment."** Kluger, "The Spark of Invention."

114 **"...such miraculous results."** Spender, in Ghiselin, 114-15.

115 **On intuition.** See Gigerenzer, *Gut Feelings.*

115 **...only rarely given.** Wakefield, 268.

116 **"...it was mostly intuition."** Emmons, in Wakefield, 268.

117 **"...be reassured, it's there."** Audette, 51.

117 **"...works of their predecessors."** Johnson, *Creators,* 4.

119 **"...surprisingly valuable experience."** Audette, 29-30.

120 **"...fear of not excelling."** Ueland, 10.

121 **"...feeling about anything."** Ueland, 6.

121 **"...we fear the most."** Ulrich, *The Widening Stream,* 8.

122 **"...from the other side."** Hall, *Conversations with Audre Lord,* 73

Chapter 6

125   "...be in your favor." Audette, 58.

126   "...generally done slowly." Ruskin, 23.

127   "...(pressure) of the environment." Rhodes, "An Analysis of Creativity."

127   "...adopt the creative product." Simonton, "Creativity, Leadership, and Chance," in Sternberg, *The Nature of Creativity*, 386-87.

129   "...not to waste time." Sarton, in Romesburg, 259.

130   "...subject at hand." Woollen, in Wakefield, 225.

130   "...as much as possible." Audette, 42.

130   "...never deviated from hard work." Miro, in Romesburg, 170.

131   "...heightened consciousness." May, 44.

132   "...relaxed, then bored." Csikszentmihalyi, *Finding Flow*, 31.

133   "...given length of time." Goldberg, in Hadden, 208.

134   "...for all the arts." Hershman, in Wakefield, 261.

134   "...your creative imagination." May, 137.

136   "...controlling the creative process." Oldach, 5.

137   "...over the process." Csikszentmihalyi, *Good Business*, 134.

137   "...likely to regret it." Csikszentmihalyi, *Good Business*, 135.

139   "...aren't very creative." Zschau, in Ray & Myers, 100.

139   "...about their worth." Mauzy & Harriman, 29.

141   "...not yet come out." Hyde, "A Conversation with Gertrude Stein," in Ghiselin, 160.

141   ...through a first draft. Block, *Writing the Novel*, 131.

Chapter 7

179   **"Failure humbles."** Tharp, 213.

180   **"...becoming a cook."** Child, *My Life in France*, 89.

181   **...on to new ideas.** Seabrook, *Flash of Genius*.

181   **"...when trouble hits."** Tharp, 222.

182   **"...refuse to deal with it."** Tharp, 218.

Chapter 8

185   **"...die of lethargy."** Chandler, in Romesburg, 194.

188   **"...alignment in this area."** Beam, 21.

189   **"...we're in balance."** Beam, 19, 21-31.

189   **"...interchange with others."** Mauzy and Harriman, 107.

190   **"...it does not need."** Grudin, 141.

Appendix I

195   **"...2% of adults score at the top."** Land and Jarman, *Breakpoint and Beyond*, citing Land's 1968 study.

196   **"...small number of resistant children."** Torrance, 171-72.

197   **"...as they grow older."** L'Engle, 53.

197   **Multiple intelligences.** Originally theorized in Gardner (1993), later updated in Gardner (2008). See also https://multipleintelligencesoasis.org/the-components-of-mi.

198   **"...doing the judging."** Weisberg, *Creativity*, 86.

199   **"Creativity suffers."** Medina, 39.

200   **"...time, and hard work?"** Torrance, 22.

201   **"...just for a table of contents."** Toni Burbank, personal correspondence, 2011.

202 "...not raw talent alone." Weisberg, 122.

203 "...time limit on their involvement." Grudin, 13.

204 "...relationship with her child." May, 40.

205 "...how they are approached." Ulrich, xv.

207 "...to teach. Never." Barron, Montuori, and Barron, 63, 65.

207 "...he found a solution." Klein, *The Change Makers*, 36.

209 "...it just doesn't." Hadden, 42.

210 "...lifelong learners." Medina, 27.

213 Power of visualization examples, Ray and Myers, 70-71.

Appendix II

217 "...not too much wiser, either." Johnson-Laird, in Sternberg, 202.

219 "...their rules communicate." Gigerenzer, 77.

220 "...resentment of newness." Grudin, 99.

220 "...who can do the job." Schank, *The Creative Attitude*, 48.

220 "...good person every time." Robinson and Stern, 29.

221 "...intrinsic motivation for an activity." Deci, in Robinson and Stern, 54.

222 "...occur through attrition." Lockwood and Walton, 13.

224 Nucor CEO comments. See Iverson, *Plain Talk*.

225 "...it's a way of life." Anderson, Finley, and Sparks, "Nucor: Values and Transition."

226 "...tend to make better decisions." Robinson and Stern, 170.

227 "...was well done." Csikszentmihalyi, *Good Business*, 93.

228 "...will ultimately fail." Mauzy and Harriman, 179.

229 "…how they will happen." Robinson and Stern, 12.

229 "…better business performance." Mauzy and Harriman, 137 and footnote 28.

229 "…homogeneity and diversity." Ind and Watt, in Lockwood and Walton, 81.

236 "…dinky, pressy Criticalness." Ueland, 1.

237 "…either right or wrong." Schank, 318.

240 "…is not enough." Bacon, 76.

240 "…is given annually." Glick, in Lockwood and Walton, 77.

241 "…be positive, too." Bacon, 48.

241 "…themselves are transformed." Bacon, 49.

242 "…the easy answer." Ulrich, 196.

Bibliography

Adams, James L. *The Care and Feeding of Ideas*. Addison-Wesley, 1986.

Albert, Leon Battista. *On Painting*. Yale: 1966.

Aldrich, Anne Hazard. *Notes From Myself: A Guide to Creative Journaling*. Carroll & Graf, 1998.

Altshuller, Genrich. *And Suddenly the Inventor Appeared*. Translated by Lev Shulyak. Technical Innovation Center, 1984, 1992.

Amabile, Teresa M. "How to Kill Creativity." *Harvard Business Review* 76, no. 5 (Sept/Oct 1998): 76-87.

Anderson, Harold H. *Creativity and Its Cultivation*. Harper, 1959.

Anderson, S. C., R. L. Finley, and W. Sparks. "Nucor: Values and Transition." *Business Case Journal* 16, No. 2 (2009): 64-72 .

Andreasen, Nancy C. *The Creating Brain: The Neuroscience of Genius*. Dana Press, 2005.

Arieti, Silvano. *Creativity: The Magic Synthesis*. Basic Books, 1976.

Audette, Anna Held. *The Blank Canvas: Inviting the Muse*. Shambhala, 1993.

Bacon, John U. *Cirque du Soleil: The Spark*. Doubleday, 2006.

Barron, Frank, Alfonso Montuori, and Anthea Barron, eds. *Creators on Creating*. Tarcher Penguin, 1997.

Barrow, John D. *The Artful Universe*. Oxford, 1995.

Barzun, Jacques. *From Dawn to Decadence: 500 Years of Western Cultural Life*. HarperCollins, 2000.

Bayles, David and Ted Orland. *Art and Fear: Observations on the Perils (and Rewards) of Artmaking*. Capra Press, 1993.

Beam, Lisa Sonora. *The Creative Entrepreneur*. Quarry Books, 2008.

Benedict, Jeff. *No Bone Unturned: The Adventures of a Top Smithsonian Scientist and the Legal Battle for America's Oldest Skeletons*. HarperCollins, 2003.

Block, Eugene. *The Wizard of Berkeley*. Coward-McCann, 1958.

Block, Lawrence. *Writing the Novel: From Plot to Print*. Writer's Digest Books, 1979.

Bloom, Harold. *Genius*. Warner Books, 2002.

Boorstein, Daniel J. *The Creators*. Vintage, 1992, 1993.

_____. *The Discoverers*. Vintage, 1983, 1985.

_____. *The Seekers*. Vintage, 1998, 1999.

Booth, Eric. *The Everyday Work of Art*. Sourcebooks, 1997, 1999.

Brett, Simon. *Faber Book of Diaries*. Faber & Faber, 1989.

Brizendine, Louann. *The Female Brain*. Broadway, 2010.

_____. *The Male Brain*. Broadway, 2007.

Brynie, Faith H. *Brain Sense*. AMACOM, 2009.

Burke, James. *The Day the Universe Changed.* Little, Brown, 1985.

Buzan, Tony and Barry Buzan. *The Mind Map Book.* Plume, 1996.

Cameron, Julia. *The Artist's Way.* Tarcher, 1992, 2002.

_____. *Walking in This World.* Tarcher, 2002.

Catmull, Ed and Amy Davis. *Creativity Inc.* Random House: 2014.

Cepero, Helen. *Journaling as a Spiritual Practice.* IVP Books, 2008.

Child, Julia with Alex Prud'homme. *My Life in France.* Knopf, 2006.

Ciefelli, Edward M. *John Ciardi: A Biography.* University of Arkansas Press, 1998.

Clapham, Maria M. "Ideational Skills Training: A Key Element in Creativity Training Programs." *Creativity Research Journal 10,* No. 1 (1997): 33-44.

Clark, Roy Peter. *Writing Tools.* Little, Brown, 2006.

Clark, Thomas, ed. *The Basics of Writing Bestsellers: Your Guide to Writing & Selling Today's Hottest Books (Writer's Digest Guide, Vol 17).* Writer's Digest Books, 1995.

Collins, Judy. *Morning, Noon, and Night: Living the Creative Life.* TarcherPerigee, 2005.

Copland, Aaron. *What To Listen For in Music.* Signet Classic, 2002.

Craig, Emily. *Teasing Secrets from the Dead: My Investigations at America's Most Famous Crime Scenes.* Crown, 2004.

Crick, Francis. *What Mad Pursuit: A Personal View of Scientific Discovery.* Basic Books, 1990.

Csikszentmihalyi, Mihalyi. *Creativity: Flow and the Psychology of Discovery and Invention.* HarperCollins, 1996.

_____. *Finding Flow: The Psychology of Engagement with Everyday Life.* Basic Books, 1997.

_____. *Good Business: Leadership, Flow, and the Making of Meaning.* Viking, 2003.

de Bono, Edward. *de Bono's Thinking Course, revised edition.* Facts on File, 1982, 1994.

de Botton, Alain. *The Architecture of Happiness.* Hamish Hamilton, 2006.

Denning, Stephen. *Springboard: How Storytelling Ignites Action in Knowledge-Era Organization.* Butterworth-Heinemann, 2000.

_____. "Telling Tales." *Harvard Business Review* 82, No. 5 (May 2004): 122-29.

Dickens, Charles. The Letters of Charles Dickens, Vol. 2, 1857-1870. Chapman and Hall, 1880.

Dimnet, Ernest. *The Art of Thinking.* Simon & Schuster, 1928.

Dreyfuss, Henry. *Designing for People.* Allworthy, 1955, 2003.

Duncker, Karl. "On Problem-Solving." *Psychological Monographs 58*, No. 5 (1945).

Edwards, Betty. *Drawing on the Artist Within.* Fireside Book, 1987.

_____. *The New Drawing on the Right Side of the Brain.* Tarcher Penguin, 1979, 1999.

Fletcher, Ralph. *A Writer's Notebook.* HarperCollins, 1996, 2003.

Flinchum, Russell. *Henry Dreyfuss, Industrial Designer: The Man in the Brown Suit.* Rizzoli, 1997.

Flora, Carlin. "Everyday Creativity." *Psychology Today,* Nov/Dec 2009, 62-73.

Florida, Richard. *The Rise of the Creative Class.* Basic Books, 2002, 2004.

Fontenot, Nancy A. "Effects of Training in Creativity and Creative Problem Finding Upon Business People." *Journal of Social Psychology 133,* No. 1 (1992): 11-22.

Fritz, Robert. *Creating.* Fawcett Columbine, 1991.

Gardner, Howard. *Creating Minds.* Basic Books, 1993.

_____. *5 Minds for the Future.* Harvard Business Press, 2008.

Ghiselin, Brewster, ed. *The Creative Process.* New American Library, 1952.

Gigerenzer, Gerd. *Gut Feelings: The Intelligence of the Unconscious.* Penguin, 2007.

Goleman, Daniel, Paul Kaufman, and Michael Ray. *The Creative Spirit.* Plume, 1993.

Grafton, Sue. "The Use of the Journal in a Private Eye Novel." In *Writing the Private Eye Novel,* edited by Robert Randisi. Writers Digest Books, 1997.

Grudin, Robert. *The Grace of Great Things: Creativity and Innovation.* Mariner Books, 1990.

Hadden, Peggy. *The Artist's Quest of Inspiration.* Allworth, 2004.

Hall, Joan Wylie. *Conversations with Audre Lorde*. University Press of Mississippi, 2004.

Hermann, Ned. *The Creative Brain*. Brain Books, 1989, 1990.

Holzer, Burghild Nina. *A Walk Between Heaven and Earth*. Three Rivers, 1994.

Iverson, Ken. *Plain Talk: Lessons from a Business Maverick*. Wiley, 1997.

Jacobs, Charles S. *Management Rewired: Why Feedback Doesn't Work and Other Surprising Lessons from the Latest Brain Science*. Portfolio Trade, 2009.

Jennings, Maureen. *The Map of Your Mind*. McClelland & Stewart, 2001.

Johnson, Alexandra. *The Hidden Writer: Diaries and the Creative Life*. Anchor Books, 1997.

_____. *Leaving A Trace: On Keeping a Journal*. Little, Brown, 2001.

Johnson, Paul. *Creators*. HarperCollins, 2006.

Kaufman, Natalie Hevener and Carol McGinnis Kay. *"G" Is for Grafton: The World of Kinsey Millhone*. Henry Holt, 1997.

Kent, Corita and Jan Steward. *Learning By Heart: Teachings to Free the Creative Spirit*. Bantam, 1992.

King, Stephen. *On Writing: A Memoir of the Craft*. Scribner, 2000.

Klein, Maury. *The Change Makers: From Carnegie to Gates*. Times Books, 2003.

Klug, Ronald. *How to Keep a Spiritual Journal*. Augsburg, 1982, 1993.

Kluger, Jeffrey, "The Spark of Invention." *Time,* November 14, 2013.

Koestler, Arthur. *The Act of Creation.* Macmillan, 1964.

Kramer, Mark and Wendy Call. *Telling True Stories.* Plume, 2007.

Lally, Phillipa, et al. "How Are Habits Formed: Modelling Habit Formation in the Real World." *European Journal of Social Psychology 40,* No. 6 (October 2010): 998-1009.

Land, George and Beth Jarman. *Breakpoint and Beyond: Mastering the Future Today.* HarperCollins, 1993.

Lamott, Anne. *Bird by Bird: Some Instructions on Writing and Life.* Anchor, 1995.

Langer, Ellen J. *The Power of Mindful Learning.* Addison Wesley, 1997.

Le Guin, Ursula K. *Steering the Craft.* The Eighth Mountain Press, 1998.

Lewis, C. S. *A Mind Awake.* Mariner Books, 2003.

L'Engle, Madeleine. *Walking on Water.* Shaw, 2001.

Lockwood, Thomas and Thomas Walton, eds. *Corporate Creativity: Developing an Innovative Organization.* Allworth Press: 2008.

MacKenzie, Gordon. *Orbiting the Giant Hairball: A Corporate Fool's Guide to Surviving with Grace.* Viking Penguin, 1998.

Mallon, Thomas. *A Book of One's Own: People and Their Diaries.* Penguin, 1984.

Marcus Aurelius. *The Emperor's Handbook.* Translated by C. S. Hicks and D. V. Hicks. Scribner, 2002.

Mauzy, Jeff and Richard Harriman. *Creativity, Inc.: Building an Inventive Organization.* Harvard Business School Press, 2003.

May, Rollo. *The Courage to Create.* W. W. Norton, 1975.

Medina, John. *Brain Rules.* Pear Press, 2008.

Michalko, Michael. *Cracking Creativity: The Secrets of Creative Genius.* 10 Speed Press, 2001.

_____. *Thinkertoys: A Handbook of Creative Thinking Techniques, 2nd edition.* 10 Speed Press, 1991, 2006.

Moore, Thomas. *The Re-Enchantment of Everyday Life.* HarperCollins, 1996.

Muller, Wayne. *Sabbath: Restoring the Sacred Rhythm of Rest.* Bantam, 1999.

Murray, Donald. *Creating A Life in Essay, Story, Poem.* Boynton/Cook, 1996.

Nalebuff, Barry & Ian Ayres. *Why Not?* Harvard Business School Press, 2003, 2006.

Nayak, P. Ranganath and John M. Kettingham. *Breakthroughs!* Rawson Associates, 1986.

New York Times. *Writers on Writing: Collected Essays.* Times Books, 2001.

Norman, Donald A. *The Psychology of Everyday Things.* Basic Books, 1988.

Oldach, Mark. *Creativity for Graphic Designers.* North Light Books, 1995.

Orland, Ted. *The View from the Studio Door.* Image Continuum, 2006.

Osbon, Diane K., ed. *Reflections on the Art of Living: A Joseph Campbell Companion.* Harper Collins, 1991.

Osborn, Alex. *Your Creative Power.* Scribner's, 1948, 1988.

Pascal, Eugene. *Jung to Live By: A Guide to the Practical Application of Jungian Principles for Everyday Life.* Warner Books, 1992.

Paterson, Katherine. *A Sense of Wonder: On Reading and Writing Fiction for Children.* Plume, 1981, 1995.

Peters, Thomas J. and Robert H. Waterman, Jr. *In Search of Excellence: Lessons from America's Best-Run Companies.* Warner Books, 1982.

Pickard, Nancy and Lynn Lott. *Seven Steps on the Writer's Path.* Ballantine, 2004.

Pink, Daniel. *A Whole New Mind.* Riverhead Books, 2005.

_____. *Drive.* Riverhead Books, 2009.

Pinker, Steven. *How the Mind Works.* Norton, 1997.

Pressfield, Steven. *The War of Art.* Grand Central, 2002.

Raab, Diana M., ed. *Writers and Their Notebooks.* University of South Carolina Press, 2010

Rainer, Tristine. *The New Diary.* Jeremy Tarcher, 1978.

Raudsepp, Eugene. *How Creative Are You?* Perigee, 1981.

Ray, Michael and Rochelle Myers. *Creativity in Business.* Doubleday, 1986.

Rhodes, Mel. "An analysis of creativity." *The Phi Delta Kappan* 42, No. 7 (1961): 305-310.

Rilke, Rainer Maria. *Letters to a Young Poet.* Translated by Stephen Mitchell. Vintage, 1986.

Robinson, Alan G. and Sam Stern. *Corporate Creativity: How Innovation and Improvement Actually Happens.* Berrett Koehler, 1997.

Romesburg, H. Charles. *The Life of the Creative Spirit*. XLibris, 2001.

Root-Bernstein, Robert and Michèle Root-Bernstein. *Sparks of Genius: The 13 Thinking Tools of the World's Most Creative People*. Houghton Mifflin, 1999.

Rosenthal, Lisa, ed. *The Writing Group Book: Creating and Sustaining a Successful Writing Group*. Chicago Review Press, 2003.

Rosner, Stanley and Lawrence E. Abt, eds. *The Creative Experience*. Grossman, 1970.

Ruskin, John. *The Elements of Drawing*. Smith, Elder, 1857.

Sark. *A Creative Companion: How to free your creative spirit*. Celestial Arts, 1991.

Schank, Roger with Peter Childers. *The Creative Attitude*. Macmillan, 1988.

Schwartz, Jeffrey M. and Sharon Begley. *The Mind and the Brain: Neuroplasticity and the Power of Mental Force*. HarperCollins, 2002.

Shekerjian, Denise. *Uncommon Genius: How Great Ideas Are Born*. Penguin, 1990.

Simonton, Dean Keith. "Exceptional Personal Influence: An Integrative Paradigm." *Creativity Research Journal 8*, No. 4 (1995): 371–376.

Seabrook, John. *Flash of Genius*. Griffin, 2008.

Solnit, Rebecca. *Wanderlust: A History of Walking*. Viking, 2000.

Stacey, Ralph D. *Complexity and Creativity in Organizations*. Berrett Koehler, 1996.

Stanislavki, Constantin. *An Actor Prepares.* Theatre Arts Books, 1936, 1948.

Sternberg, Robert J. *The Nature of Creativity.* Cambridge University Press, 1988.

Sussman, Aaron & Ruth Goode. *The Magic of Walking.* Simon & Schuster, 1967, 1969.

Taylor, Irene and Alan Taylor. *The Assassin's Cloak: An Anthology of the World's Greatest Diarists.* Canongate UK, 2011.

Tharp, Twyla with Mark Reiter. *The Creative Habit.* Simon & Schuster, 2003.

Toms, Michael, et al. *The Well of Creativity.* New Dimensions, 1997.

Torrance, E. Paul. *The Search for Satori & Creativity.* Creative Education Foundation, 1979.

Ueland, Brenda. *If You Want to Write.* Gray Wolf Press, 1938, 1987.

Ulrich, David. *The Widening Stream: The Seven Stages of Creativity.* Beyond Words Publishing, 2002.

Vamos, Mark N. and David Lidsky. *Fast Company's Greatest Hits.* Penguin, 2006.

van Doren, Charles. *A History of Knowledge.* Ballantine, 1991.

von Oech, Roger. *A Kick in the Seat of the Pants.* Harper, 1986.

_____. *A Whack on the Side of the Head.* Warner Books, 1983.

Wakefield, Dan. *Creating from the Spirit: A Path to Creative Power in Art and Life.* Ballantine, 1996.

Wallace, Doris B. and Howard E. Gruber. *Creative People at Work.* Oxford, 1989.

Watson, James D. *The Double Helix: A Personal Account of the Discovery of the Structure of DNA*. Touchstone, 2001.

Weihs, Karen M. *Out of My Mind*. Five Corners, 1999.

Weisberg, Robert W. *Creativity: Genius and Other Myths*. Freeman & Co., 1986.

West, Thomas G. *In the Mind's Eye*. Prometheus Books, 1997.

White, Michael. *Acid Tongues and Tranquil Dreamers: Tales of Bitter Rivalry That Fueled the Advancement of Science and Technology*. William Morrow, 2001.

Whyte, David. *The Heart Aroused: Poetry and the Preservation of the Soul of Corporate America*. Currency Doubleday, 1994.

Woolf, Virginia. *A Room of One's Own*. Harcourt Brace & Co., 1929, 1989.

Zelinski, Ernie. *The Joy of Thinking Big*. Ten Speed Press, 1998.

Acknowledgements

A separate book would be required to name all those who've shown me what "creative" looks like.

Among those who have particularly touched this book at some point in its long development are:

- The amazing students in the creativity classes in the McColl School of Business at Queens University of Charlotte. They opened themselves up to experiences and shared their frustrations, fears, and breakthroughs. Without them, this book simply wouldn't exist. I wish I could name each of you—but you know who you are.

- Loyd Dillon, artist extraordinaire, who brought to each class not only his smiley face tie and Thonet chairs but his boundless creative energy (and his story about the little artist and her purple-leafed tree, mentioned herein) and to the other special artist/teachers who shared their life-long passion with those exploring for the first time.

- Meg Ruley and Christina Hogrebe, who had faith in this early on; Toni Burbank, whose vision and experience helped shape it; and Kendel Lynn for her generosity and sound advice.

- The guys from the Mecklenburg County Jail creative writing class and their boundless creative energy.

- Jeremy Bishop and his Rookie Year poetry chapbook, Bryan

Harris and his traditional detective novel set entirely in a prison, and Andrew Hostetler, Randall Newkirk, and Edward Belton, all finding their own creative paths.

- The ladies of Dove's Nest, who in recovery are willing to come to class each week to take risks, to play—and maybe remember they really are wildly creative.

- My writer friends Paula Connolly, Dawn Cotter, Terry Hoover, and Ann Wicker, who taught me the power and the need for "tweak," and whose work has taught me much about my own. (How many drafts of this book did you all read?).

- Paul Reali for his energy and expertise in creativity and for editing a book that looks like a creativity book should look.

- All the writers I've met over the years who've taught me what a gracious, inclusive, encouraging community of creatives looks like, including those at Charlotte Lit, in Sisters in Crime, and in Mystery Writers of America.

- My amazing and crazy-creative family—Dad, Mom, sisters, nephews, brothers-in-law.

- And my husband Bob, who has gone on every adventure, no matter how zany.

About the Author

A lawyer and professor emerita in the McColl School of Business at Queens University of Charlotte, Cathy Pickens is a frequent speaker for both business and arts organizations. She offers workshops on developing the creative process, coaches and teaches writers through Charlotte Lit, and works with former prison inmates and those in rehab on telling their stories.

Southern Fried, the first of Cathy's five mystery novels, won St. Martin's Malice Domestic Award for Best Traditional Mystery. In addition, she has published legal and academic books, articles, business cases, and essays in several books on writing craft.

Her recent books include crime stories for History Press: *Charleston Mysteries, Charlotte True Crime Stories,* and *True Crime Stories of Eastern North Carolina.*

Cathy has served as president and board member of Sisters in Crime, at-large director for Mystery Writers of America, and president of the regional Forensic Medicine board.

Find Cathy on the web and contact her at cathypickens.com.

CPSIA information can be obtained
at www.ICGtesting.com
Printed in the USA
LVHW091313170920
666053LV00009B/224